FROM STIMULUS
TO SCIENCE

FROM
STIMULUS
TO
SCIENCE

W. V. Quine

Harvard University Press
Cambridge, Massachusetts
London, England
1995

Library of Congress Cataloging-in-Publication Data

Quine, W. V. (Willard Van Orman)
From stimulus to science / W. V. Quine.
p.   cm.
Includes bibliographical references and index.
ISBN 0-674-32635-0 (alk. paper)
1. Philosophy.   2. Quine, W. V. (Willard Van Orman)   I. Title.
B945.Q54A3   1995
191—dc20   95-14062

PREFACE

THE FERRATER MORA LECTURES are a semiannual event
at the Universitat de Girona, in Catalonia, honoring the memory of the late philosopher and novelist Josep María Ferrater
Mora. The lecturer meets a selected group of some forty
auditors ten times, over a period of two weeks, for a total of
twenty-odd hours of lectures and discussion. Four eminent
colleagues are invited along with the lecturer to participate in
the discussion.

I gave the lectures in November 1990, under the title "From
Stimulus to Science." My four discussants were my good friends
Donald Davidson, Burton Dreben, Dagfinn Føllesdal, and Roger
Gibson. I lectured from copious notes, and after some time I
resolved to develop them into a book. I took my time, giving
my thoughts free rein. The book is thus more an outgrowth
of the lectures than a record of them, and it is the better for
that. In addition, more than half of the lecture "Assuming
Objects," which I gave at the Royal Swedish Academy in November 1993 on receiving the Rolf Schock prize, has been
absorbed piecemeal into Chapters II, III, and VII.

I am grateful to Professor Josep María Terricabras, the genial
and solicitous director of the lectureship, for choosing me for
the occasion, for enriching it by adding the four confederates

of my choosing, and for guiding my wife and me through the ancient and medieval delights of Catalonia, eminent among which is Girona itself. As usual I am much indebted to Burt Dreben, who read the manuscript meticulously and precipitated many improvements.

W. V. Q.
March 1995

CONTENTS

FROM STIMULUS
TO SCIENCE

DAYS OF YORE

WE AND OTHER ANIMALS notice what goes on around us. This helps us by suggesting what we might expect and even how to prevent it, and thus fosters survival. However, the expedient works only imperfectly. There are surprises, and they are unsettling. How can we tell when we are right? We are faced with the problem of error.

These are worries about our knowledge of the external world. To deal with them we have had to turn inward and seek knowledge *of* knowledge. "Know thyself": the injunction is attributed to Socrates and even to Thales, purportedly the father of philosophy.

Thales and his successors were concerned not only with man and his errors; they speculated on the cosmos. But anxiety over the problem of error continued through Greek antiquity. The paradoxes of Zeno and Eubulides were calculated to show the limitations of our judgment, as were the sophistries of the Sophists. The Skeptics took the melancholy conclusions to heart.

How do we know things? Plato held that we do so by apprehending *ideas*—really forms, as we would say—that are the essences of things. He thought we were born knowing these forms and their interrelations in a blurred way, and that they could be brought into focus by Socratic dialogue. It seems from one of the dialogues, the *Meno,* that Plato arrived at this theory by thinking about mathematical argumentation from self-evident truths. Somehow, though, he accommodated observation too. "Save the appearances," he wrote.

Aristotle tried to shore up the ways of knowing. He formalized the syllogism. Knowledge itself, however, outpaced knowledge about knowledge. Natural history throve in Aristotle's hands, and mathematics in those of Eudoxus and Euclid. Eratosthenes even calculated the size of the earth, nearly enough.

But darkness descended, and mists of myth and mysticism settled in for a thousand years. Ways of knowing dwindled to one: higher authority. Remnants from Aristotle were deemed authoritative, but how had *he* known? Infinite regress loomed.

The problem was shelved by positing supernatural revelation. This position was a stubborn one, for we cannot then question divine revelation without begging the question.

Roger Bacon did beg it, along about 1290, by espousing observation and experiment. Two and a half centuries later, Copernicus made the breakthrough that put science unmistakably on the upward track. For fourteen centuries straggling astronomers had struggled with Ptolemaic epicycles to systematize an astronomy centered on the earth; but at last Copernicus put our planet in its place and set it moving.

Thus inspired, Francis Bacon took up the old question of the ways of knowing. The spirit of Roger Bacon was reawakened, but now with more substance and sophistication, the wisdom of hindsight. Science had broken through, though traditionalists tried to restrain it. A full century after Copernicus, the clergy prosecuted Galileo for embracing the Copernican heresy. One thinks of the creationists today, one hundred thirty years after Darwin's *Origin of Species.*

Despite obstructions, science attained full flower fifty years after Galileo's work. It flowered in Newton's *Philosophiae Naturalis Principia Mathematica* (1687).

In the more broadly philosophical arena, meanwhile, there was Thomas Hobbes. He was twenty-four years younger than Galileo, and was inspired by Galileo's strides. Hobbes professed utter materialism, indeed mechanism, like Democritus two thousand years before: there is nothing but matter in motion. Thought is motion in the brain.

Hobbes's view of knowledge was strikingly modern. Our sensations are the effects upon us of the otherwise unknowable material world. It is on these that we base our ideas about the world, and we have nothing further to go on but the meshing of the ideas.

Hobbes uses the word 'idea' in its modern sense, to mean something like a thought or a concept. He was the first to do so in English, according to the Oxford English Dictionary. It was an odd reversal of Plato's usage. For Plato ideas or forms had been reality *par excellence;* things of the material world were their imperfect counterfeits. For Hobbes and us, ideas are rather man's faltering attempt to encompass material reality.

René Descartes was Hobbes's junior by eight years. He was a dualist: he recognized both mind and matter. Descartes came to grips, more vigorously than Hobbes or Bacon, with the question of how we know. In his famous thought experiment he proceeded from scratch. He tried doubting everything, but found that he could not doubt that he was doubting. He concluded that he existed, as a mind. Then he proceeded to the existence of God. Sensing more treacherous ground there, he offered four proofs. The existence of matter then came easily: we have a clear and distinct idea of matter, and since

God is by definition good, He would not give us a clear and distinct but false idea.

Such, roughly stated, was Descartes's theory of how we know. Clear and distinct ideas are knowledge, and God-given; confused ideas are not. There are echoes here of Plato's doctrine of innate knowledge and reminiscence, and of the Hebrew and Christian doctrine of divine revelation. But the Platonic bit may have been a case of parallel inspiration rather than heritage. Plato's view was evidently inspired by mathematics, and Descartes was a mathematician.

In the five-year period 1646–1650 five neoclassical philosophers were alive: Hobbes, Descartes, Spinoza, Leibniz, and Locke. In the history of epistemology the next significant figure after Descartes is John Locke.

Locke shunned Descartes's theological epistemology. Like Hobbes, he saw knowledge in the coherence of ideas. He accepted the material world as real, but as known only tentatively by conjecture from ideas. Sense impressions, caused by the material world, implant our simple ideas; we build or abstract all other ideas from these. Contrary to Descartes, Locke repudiated innate ideas. He subscribed to the empiricist manifesto: *nihil in mente quod non prius in sensu.*

Locke did not explain how to form complex ideas of material objects, real or fictitious, on the basis of simple sense impressions. He wrote of the association of ideas by contiguity, succession, and resemblance, but this is the barest beginning of what goes into the most primitive report on the material world around us. What of our identification of an intermittently observed body as the same body? An identical body can look different over time, and different bodies can look alike. Much remained to be explained.

Bishop George Berkeley, fifty years younger than Locke, saw no cogency in Hobbes's or Locke's conjecture of a material world. Nothing exists, Berkeley held, but what is directly perceived. Nothing, therefore, but sensory patterns, or occurrences of sensory patterns? No, he was more generous than that. He admitted souls; we perceive ours. And somehow he admitted God. This done, Berkeley provides for the persistence of things irrespective of whether or when they are perceived by man or beast; for they remain faithfully perceived by God. Berkeley's disavowal of matter, then, would seem to be a matter of words.

David Hume, twenty-six years Berkeley's junior, acquiesced rather in the conclusion that there simply is no evidence for the continued existence of an object between one occasion and another of our perceiving it. The very identification of it as the same object, on the one occasion and the other, is in his view a confusion of identity with similarity.

Locke, Berkeley, and Hume were the classic British empiricists, and their pertinent writings appeared in the years 1690–1757. All three agreed that our lore about the world is a fabric of ideas based on sense impressions. Regarding the structured details of the fabric and its fabrication, all three were at a loss for the rudiments of an account. The idea idea is a frail reed.

As Wittgenstein observed, even a simple sense quality is elusive unless braced by public language. An individual might reckon many sensory events as recurrences of one quality on the strength of resemblance of each to the next, despite a substantial accumulation of slight differences. Public naming and monitoring are what arrest such drift. Random deviations of individual speakers are held within bounds by the speakers' communicating with one another. Public words anchor ideas.

Irresponsible appeal to the idea idea is still our popular

usage. The purpose of language is said to be the communication of ideas. We learn a word from our elders by associating it with the same idea, and we use it in the communication of ideas. How do we know that the words we use to express our ideas are conjuring up the same ideas in the minds of our listeners? Words and observable behavior are all we have to go on, and the idea idea provides only the illusion of an explanation.

John Horne Tooke urged the point in 1786, ten years after Hume's death.

> I only desire you to read [Locke's] essay over again with attention to see whether all that its immortal author has justly concluded will not hold equally true and clear, if you substitute the composition, &c, of *terms* wherever he has supposed a composition of ideas . . . The greatest part of Mr. Locke's essay, that is, all which relates to what he calls the abstraction, complexity, generalization, etc., of ideas, does indeed merely concern language.   (Pp. 37–38)

Tooke was a kindred spirit of his remote predecessor William of Ockham and other medieval nominalists, who had dismissed abstract objects as *flatus vocis,* vocal breeze. Tooke's was a major step toward what Richard Rorty has called the linguistic turn. If there is sense to be made of the compounding of ideas, clearer sense can be made of the compounding of language. Words, unlike ideas, are out where we can see what we are doing.

Much further freedom in the constructing of ideas—or, now, terms—was achieved by Jeremy Bentham a few years later in his theory of fictions. He observed that to explain a term we do not need to compose a synonymous phrase. We need only explain all sentences in which we propose to use the term. It is what is now called contextual definition. Bentham's motive was ontological: he wanted to be able to introduce one or another useful term without being charged with assuming some controversial object for it to designate, or objects for it to denote. The seeming object or objects could in this way be dismissed as innocent fictions.

In India there has been debate since the seventh century over whether sentences or words are the primary vehicles of meaning. Since the lexicon or *Wortschatz* is finite whereas the realm of admissible sentences, the *Satzschatz,* is boundless, a systematic guide to a language must consist of a dictionary of words and a grammar for building sentences from them. The words, on the other hand, will mostly be explained in the dictionary by their use in illustrative sentences. The goal of the whole enterprise is to inculcate facility in understanding and producing correct and useful sentences.

In learning our native language we zigzag similarly. We learn a simple sentence as a whole, and then we project a component word of it by analogy into the construction of another sentence. Nowadays an appreciation of contextual definition— Bentham's insight—has lent support to the view of sentences as the primary vehicles of meaning. It is a view that Gottlob Frege vigorously espoused a century after Bentham.

Contextual definition recurred in mathematics a few decades after Bentham's contribution, at the hands of George Boole. Boole is best known to philosophers and computer engineers as a pioneer in modern logic, but his contextual definitions were a contribution rather to the differential calculus. They are known as the method of operators. Adepts of the calculus will recognize '$(\delta^2/\delta x^2)f(x,y,z)$' as standing for a quantity in its own right, and '$\delta^2/\delta x^2$' as a prefix or operator standing for nothing in its own right. But Boole's innovation was to abbreviate a sum such as

$$\frac{\delta^2}{\delta x^2} f(x,y,z) + \frac{\delta^2}{\delta y^2} f(x,y,z) + \frac{\delta^2}{\delta z^2} f(x,y,z)$$

in the compact fashion

$$\left(\frac{\delta^2}{\delta x^2} + \frac{\delta^2}{\delta y^2} + \frac{\delta^2}{\delta z^2} \right) f(x,y,z).$$

and then manipulate it as if it stood for a sum of three genuine quantities multiplied into $f(x,y,z)$. The three operators and their ostensible sum represent fictitious quantities, to state the matter from Bentham's point of view. The expedient expedites computation, and is widely used in the differential calculus and elsewhere.

It was this very example that inspired Bertrand Russell's familiar contextual definition of the singular description '$(\imath x)Fx$':

'$G(\imath x)Fx$' for '$\exists y(Gy . \forall x(x = y . \equiv Fx))$'.

Russell tells us so, in *Principia Mathematica* (vol. 1, p. 66). Frank Ramsey hailed Russell's definition as a "paradigm of philosophical analysis." It dates from 1905, and had the same philosophical objective as Bentham's original theory of fictions itself; namely, useful idiom without embarrassing ontological implications. A singular description can be useful in a sentence even when we are not yet sure of the existence of one and only one such object as the description purports to designate.

The definition was one of the many deft contributions of Whitehead and Russell's three forbidding volumes of *Principia Mathematica*, which appeared in 1910–13. Their heroic project was to clarify the whole intricate structure of classical mathematics by deriving its principal concepts, step by step and definition after definition, from a slender basis of clear and simple primitive terms, and deriving its principal laws pari passu from a few postulates.

Such a project had seemed feasible because of the revolutionary advances in logic in the latter half of the nineteenth century, at the hands mainly of Gottlob Frege, Charles Sanders Peirce, and Giuseppe Peano. Progress in clarifying basic mathematical concepts had already been made by Richard Dedekind, George Cantor, and, again and especially, Frege and Peano. But it had remained to Russell and Whitehead to organize, refine, and extend these beginnings and integrate them into an organic and imposing whole. The economical foundation achieved in *Principia*, and further reduced by subsequent logicians, now comprises only the truth functions and quantification of elementary logic plus the two-place predicate 'ϵ' of class membership. The whole conceptual scheme of classical mathematics boils down to just that.

A philosophical concern that motivated Whitehead and Russell in part, and Frege before them, was as to the nature of mathematical knowledge and the basis of mathematical truth. The conclusion they drew was that mathematics is translatable into pure logic. They counted membership as logic. So mathematical truth is logical truth, they reasoned, and hence all of it must be logically deducible from self-evident logical truths. This is wrong, as transpires in part from Kurt Gödel's paper of 1931 and in part from findings by Russell himself away back in 1902.

This forlorn hope was not the only point of Russell and Whitehead's great undertaking. Its other objective, and its enduring value, was simply a deeper understanding of the central concepts of mathematics and their basic laws and interrelations. Their total translatability into just elementary logic and a single familiar two-place predicate, membership, is of itself a philosophical sensation. Modern logic was indispensable to this achievement. An essential factor, of a piece with modern logic, was contextual definition.

Buoyed by their achievement, Russell reflected in 1914 on realizing the dream of empiricist epistemologists: the explicit construction of the external world, or a reasonable facsimile, from sense impressions, hence from simple ideas. He adumbrated it in *Our Knowledge of the External World,* and a dozen years later Rudolf Carnap was undertaking to carry it out. Carnap's effort found expression in *Der logische Aufbau der Welt* (1928).

Carnap's building blocks were to be sensory elements, as in the constructions dreamed of by the old British empiricists. But what sensory elements? Atomic sense data? The Gestalt psychologists claimed that we are first aware of various organized wholes, and then we abstract the atoms. Carnap circumvented that issue by settling for unorganized global experiences. Each of his elements was the individual's total experience at the moment, or perhaps during the specious present. These global units he called *elementary experiences.*

Carnap's basic relation between elementary experiences was *remembering as similar.* I shall call it *R.* One elementary experience, *x,* bears *R* to another, *y,* if *x* includes a memory of *y* as partially resembling *x.*

Here, as in *Principia Mathematica,* economy was part of the game. Carnap allowed himself free use of logic and mathematics, and in addition just one further two-place predicate, the one I am calling *R.* He does not need to assume a further predicate to denote the elementary experiences, for he can define it: an elementary experience is anything that bears *R* to anything, or to which anything bears *R.* This can be expressed in terms of *R* and logic. Next he defines part similarity of elementary experiences: it holds if one of them bears R to the other, forward or backward. This definition would seem to deliver not just "part similar," but "remembered as part similar"; but let us pass over that.

By a more subtle definition Carnap introduces what he calls *similarity circles.* A similarity circle is any largest class of elementary experiences each of which is part-similar to each. It is largest in the sense that no elementary experience outside the class is similar to every member. All this goes easily into his growing formal notation.

This brings him to the point where he can define the notion of a sense quality. This definition well displays Carnap's ingenuity. He sets his sights on *quality classes,* a quality class being the class of all the elementary experiences that represent a given quality. All the elementary experiences in a quality class are part-similar, by virtue of sharing the quality. Still the class will be narrower than a similarity circle, for the members of a similarity circle need not all share any one quality. But Carnap argues that a quality class will always be the common part of all the similarity circles that it overlaps by more than half. This works out, he argues, if experience is reasonably varied and random. He thus arrives at a definition of quality class, wholly within his formalism. Finally he just identifies qualities with the quality classes. This move, which Carnap calls quasi-analysis, plays a major role in the *Aufbau.*

Carnap then goes on to define similarity of qualities, exploiting part similarity of elementary experiences. Given that, he manages to define the five senses: sight, smell, taste, hearing, and touch. Each sense is a largest class of qualities that are connected each to each by chains of similarity. The five senses are separated from one another by breaks in the chains; no visual quality is similar to any auditory one. Finally, each of the five senses can be singled out by its dimensionality; for, Carnap points out, each has a different number of dimensions. Sight, for instance, has five: the two spatial dimensions of the visual field and the three dimensions of color (hue, brilliance, saturation). Dimension itself is definable mathematically, hence ultimately by logic and membership.

Why all these ingenious and laborious constructions? Carnap wanted to identify the minimum essential determinants of sense experience. He was making it plausible that one might go on in this way and single out, by definition, every sense quality and every visual position. Given this full sensory foundation, then, he would undertake the great project of somehow building upon it our full system of physical reality.

He envisaged, as a first step in that construction, a projection of the visual qualities of our two-dimensional visual field into three-dimensional space. Imagine lines projected outward from all points in the rounded front of the subject's eye. Each line is perpendicular to its immediate neighborhood on that rounded surface. Each is the subject's line of sight from that point on the eye, and thus corresponds to a point in the subject's visual field. The color of that point in the visual field is to be assigned to a point on that line of sight, out in three-dimensional space. Colors are to be assigned in this way to all the lines of sight, one color to each. The remaining question is, how far out on each line?

Those distances are to be so adjusted, Carnap answers, as to minimize the variegation of color in the resulting three-dimensional space. And not only that; we must try also to minimize or retard the change of color over time at each point, thus going back and readjusting earlier assignments in the light of later input. In short, we are so to assign colors to points in space-time as to make for the drabbest and slowest possible world. A law of least action gets built into our very standard of what to count as real. This was a deep insight of Carnap's. It is a stick-figure caricature of what the scientist actually does, early and late, in devising theories. It is the scientist's quest of the simplest solution.

Carnap's construction of the sensory domain was strictly by definition, as far as it went, and he gave reason to believe that that job could be completed by further definition on the same basis. For the subsequent construction of the physical world, however, one could not hope to proceed purely by definition; for minimization requires us to go back and reconsider past spatial allocations of qualities in the light of later ones. We are given a canon of procedure, and a brilliant one, but not one that makes the theory of the external world translatable into the language of sense experience. That is too much to ask.

Carnap's *Aufbau* was the culmination of the phenomenalism that evolved through Hobbes, Locke, Berkeley, and Hume and had had its roots in Descartes's doubts and in the ancient perplexity over knowledge and error. Yet Carnap's motivation was not this traditional quest for certainty. Rather, his goal was just a systematic integration—what he called a "constitution system"—of our scientific concepts of mind and nature. Whitehead and Russell gave us the construction of mathematics from minimal beginnings; Carnap went on from there, accepting logic and mathematics as a finished tool for use in his further constructions. His choice of experiences rather than physical objects as his foundation was, he assures us, just a matter of strategy.

Even so, Carnap's inspiration was only in part *Principia Mathematica*. It was more emphatically Russell's frankly epistemological *Our Knowledge of the External World*. Thus it is that his constitution system took the form of a "rational reconstruction"—Carnap's phrase again—of man's conceptual development. If by 1928 he was seeing this rational reconstruction as merely a good strategy for a constitution system of global science, still there is no mistaking the epistemological predilection that led him to it.

❧ II ❧

NATURALISM

THE IDEA of a self-sufficient sensory language as a foundation for science loses its lustre when we reflect that systematization of our sensory intake is the very business that science itself is engaged in. The memories that link our past experiences with present ones and induce our expectations are themselves mostly memories not of sensory intake but of essentially scientific posits, namely things and events in the physical world. It was perhaps appreciation of this point that led Otto Neurath, Carnap's colleague in Vienna, to persuade Carnap to give up his methodological phenomenalism in favor of physicalism.

Though Carnap had represented the phenomenalistic orientation of his "rational reconstruction" as a pragmatic choice without metaphysical significance, Neurath probably saw it (and I do) as embracing a Cartesian dualism of mind and body, if not indeed a mentalistic monism. Physicalism, on the other hand, is materialism, bluntly monistic except for the abstract objects of mathematics.

Carnap did not then switch to the purported pragmatic alternative of a physically based constitution system for science. He turned instead to quite other lines in the philosophy and logic of science. He refused for decades to permit an English edition of the *Aufbau.*

If that physicalistic alternative were to be pursued, two directions suggest themselves. One, aimed solely at conceptual economy and clarity in the spirit of *Principia Mathematica,* is pretty much what physicists at the theoretical pole have long been up to, though the logician might lend a welcome hand in the trimming and polishing before the final miniaturized model is cast in bronze. The other direction, more analogous to Carnap's *Aufbau,* is what I think of as *naturalism.* It is rational reconstruction of the individual's and/or the race's actual acquisition of a responsible theory of the external world. It would address the question how we, physical denizens of the physical world, can have projected our scientific theory of that whole world from our meager contacts with it: from the mere impacts of rays and particles on our surfaces and a few odds and ends such as the strain of walking uphill.

Such is my option. It is part and parcel of empirical science itself, with rational reconstruction intruding only at the conjectural interstices or where complexities of historical accident becloud the schematic understanding we are seeking. The motivation is still philosophical, as motivation in natural science tends indeed to be, and the inquiry proceeds in disregard of disciplinary boundaries but with respect for the disciplines themselves and appetite for their input. Unlike the old epistemologists, we seek no firmer basis for science than science itself; so we are free to use the very fruits of science in investigating its roots. It is a matter, as always in science, of tackling one problem with the help of our answers to others.

Despite this radical shift in orientation and goal, we can imitate the phenomenalistic groundwork of Carnap's *Aufbau* in our new setting. His ground elements were his elementary experiences; each was the subject's total sensory experience during some moment, or specious present. What can we take as the physical analogue? Simply the class of all sensory receptors that were triggered at that moment; or, better, the temporally ordered class of receptors triggered during that specious present. The input gets processed in the brain, but what distinguishes one unvarnished input from another is just what receptors were triggered and in what order. Here is a fitting physical correlate of the global sensory experience of a moment. I call it a *global stimulus*.

So global stimuli—ordered sets of receptors—are what I propose as physical analogues of Carnap's elementary experiences. And what then of his relation *R*, as I called it, of remembered part similarity? To set my analogy rolling, let me drop the memory factor here and settle for just part similarity: the relation of two elementary experiences such that part of one resembles part of the other. My physical analogue, then, is *perceptual similarity*, seen as a relation between global stimuli.

Though physical, this relation is not to be confused with a more obvious kind of similarity between global stimuli. Each global stimulus is an ordered subset of the subject's nerve endings, and two such subsets are more or less similar in the obvious sense according as they comprise more or less the same nerve endings in more or less the same order. This I call *receptual* similarity.

Perceptual similarity, on the other hand, is a matter rather of effect on the subject: a question of reaction. Two receptually very similar global stimuli are indeed apt to be perceptually similar, but two receptually very dissimilar ones can be perceptually similar too; for many of the receptors triggered on a given occasion are indifferent to the response.

An individual's standards of perceptual similarity, at any

given stage of his development, are in principle objectively testable, as follows. The individual happens to make some move on the occasion of some global stimulation, and we reward the move. Later we stimulate him again in a receptually somewhat similar way, and in view of the past reward he makes the same move again, but this time we penalize it. Finally we stimulate him again, this time in a way intermediate between the two stimulations, in respect of receptive similarity. If he makes the move a third time, despite the recent penalty, we conclude that the third stimulation was perceptually more similar to the first than to the second.

My purpose in focusing on nerve endings, rather than more distant features of the physical world, is of course to narrow our sights to the limited physical contacts on which our theory of the world is based. But we noted that even these global stimuli are excessive: most of the receptors triggered on any occasion are perceptually ineffective. What matter are the *salient* ones. We can now proceed to narrow our sights to these, for salience is definable in terms of receptual and perceptual similarity. The receptors that make for salience within a global stimulus are the ones that the stimulus shares with other global stimuli to which it is perceptually similar but receptually dissimilar. The salient part is the part by virtue of which the global stimulus is perceptually similar to others despite divergence of other parts.

Intuitively, the global stimuli are perceptually similar by virtue of the shared salience. Experimentally and definitionally, it is the perceptual similarity and receptual dissimilarity of the global stimuli that constitute the shared salience. The inversion is in the spirit of Carnap's constructions.

Salience is the operative factor in ostensive definition. Motion enhances salience, and sweeping or pointing gestures in the vicinity or direction of the intended portion of the scene thus implements the desired association with the spoken word.

Salience enables us to sort out the sense modalities. A global stimulus is visual or auditory according as its salient receptors are in the retina or the cochlea; and correspondingly for the other modalities. It is the global stimulus, still, that I assign to this or that modality according to where the salience lies. Here again I sense the spirit of Carnap's *Aufbau*.

Perceptual similarity diverges from receptual similarity not only on the score of salience. Thus consider a rectangle, flat on the floor and viewed consecutively from various angles, always saliently. The stimuli will be dissimilar receptually, for the retinal projection of the rectangle will range from a rectangle to various extremes of trapezoid and parallelogram. Still they will be perceptually similar, for we have a learned or instinctive propensity to associate perspectives.

I have come this far in my physical mimicry of phenomenalistic epistemology without invading the percipient organism more deeply than his sensory receptors. All that has mattered is the individual's distinctive responses to their activation. I shall not have to invade him more deeply, despite the illuminating progress of psychoneurology.

Perceptual similarity is the basis of all expectation, all learning, all habit formation. It operates through our propensity to expect perceptually similar stimulations to have sequels perceptually similar to each other. This is primitive induction.

Since learning hinges thus on perceptual similarity, perceptual similarity cannot itself have been learned—not all of it. Some of it is innate. One's standards of perceptual similarity change radically, however, and perhaps rapidly for a while, in consequence of experience and learning.

The survival value of primitive induction is anticipation of something edible, or of some creature by which one might be eaten. Thus it is that natural selection has endowed us with standards of perceptual similarity that mesh pretty well with natural trends, affording us better than random success in our expectations. Thus it is that induction has been serving us and other animals so well. The future is as may be, but we persist hopefully.

Evolution has further favored some of us animals, notably birds, apes, and humans, with the means of widening our horizons by the sharing of information. Birds have their calls and apes their cries.

Apes have a repertoire of distinct signals for distinct purposes. One signal warns the fellow apes of the approach of a lion or leopard, another warns of an eagle, another perhaps reports the sighting of some fruit trees while the troop is ranging through the forest. Each distinctive cry has become keyed to some distinctive range of stimulations, whether by instinct or conditioning. Each member of the tribe is disposed to broadcast the appropriate signal on undergoing any one of a certain range of perceptually fairly similar global stimulations, and to react with appropriate motor behavior on hearing the signal.

There is a puzzle here. Global stimuli are private: each is a temporally ordered set of some one individual's receptors. Their perceptual similarity, in part innate and in part molded by experience, is private as well. Whence then this coordination of behavior across the tribe? It requires that if two individuals jointly witness one scene, and subsequently jointly witness another scene, and the one witness's global stimulations on the two occasions qualify for him as perceptually similar, usually the other witness's stimulations will so qualify for the other witness.

The same is required of the signal. Recurrences of it must

activate, in each individual, global stimuli that are perceptually similar for that individual.

So we see a preestablished harmony of perceptual similarity standards. If two scenes trigger perceptually similar global stimuli in one witness, they are apt to do likewise in another.

This public harmony of private standards of perceptual similarity is accounted for by natural selection. The individual's initial standards of perceptual similarity are inculcated, we saw, by natural selection, and so, thanks to shared ancestry and shared environment, will tend to harmonize across the tribe. The changes in standards subsequent to birth will also tend to harmonize, because of the shared society and environment. There is also the discipline imposed by the vocal signals themselves and, later, language: random deviation among individuals gets correctively canceled out by their hearing the signals from one another.

A page or two back I commented on creatures being *disposed* to broadcast signals on appropriate occasions. I shall appeal freely to dispositions. We do so when we say what one *would* do, or what *would* happen, *if.* What then is a disposition? It is just one or another physical property, one or another trait of the internal structure or composition of the disposed object or related objects. The seeming difference between dispositions and other physical properties resides merely in our way of specifying them. We call a property a disposition if we specify it by citing a symptom, or test. The paradigm of dispositions, solubility in water, is a recondite matter of microscopic structure, but it is one that we conveniently specify by just citing a symptom or test: the substance will dissolve on immersion. The disposition of an ape or bird to broadcast the appropriate signal is again a physical trait, something to do with the organization of the creature's neural network.

To resume, then. I was back with the birds and the apes,

and I now move on to man. What I call *observation sentences* are, at their most primitive, the human counterparts of bird-calls and apes' cries. Examples are 'It's raining', 'It's cold', 'Dog!'. They are occasion sentences—true on some occasions, false on others. Furthermore they report intersubjectively observable situations, observable outright. That is to say, all members of the language community are disposed to agree on the truth or falsity of such a sentence on the spot, if they have normal perception and are witnesses to the occasion.

The pertinent language community is a parameter that we may take more broadly or narrowly according to the purpose of our study. Also there is vagueness to allow for. How many seconds of reflection does 'outright' permit? Or again, take 'Swan!' or 'Lo, a swan': would our speaker affirm it of a black one? He would hesitate and go one way or the other, or just be stymied, though within familiar ground it is an observation sentence. However, we can get on best by exploiting the notion of observation sentence as if it were well defined, while keeping these gradations in the back of our minds.

Within the individual the observation sentence is keyed to a range of perceptually fairly similar global stimuli, as are the birdcalls and the apes' cries in individual birds and apes. It is thanks to the preestablished harmony, again, that they qualify as observation sentences across the community. The harmony is responsible for all language and its precursors, right back to birds and apes.

Our observation sentences are not only our counterparts of those prehuman harbingers of language, they are the inception of language. They are its inception not only prehistorically, as I presume them to be, but also currently with the recruitment of each new child into the language community. They are the child's entering wedge into cognitive language, for they are the expressions that can be conditioned to global stimuli without the aid of prior language. Some of them, such as 'Milk!' and 'Dog!', are what we in our sophistication see as terms denoting things, but to the child, innocent at first of any thought of reification and reference, they are on a par with 'It's cold' and 'It's raining': just things to say in distinctive circumstances. Hence I call them all sentences.

The child learns its first observation sentences, we see, by ostension, in a somewhat extended sense of the term; that is, under global stimulations having appropriate salient features or traits that are not verbal in turn. But already at an early age the child has swiftly amassed a repertoire of observation sentences beyond all compare with bird or ape. He is innately more agile at learning new observation sentences by ostension, and beyond this soon learns connectives by which to compound new observation sentences from old ones. 'Not' and 'and' come to mind. A negative observation sentence, 'Not p', is probably first learned when the child's mentor utters it as a correction, the child having wrongly affirmed the underlying observation sentence 'p'. The connective 'and' is a painless acquisition, amounting as it does to the merest punctuation between affirmations. But, despite its triviality, 'and' proves productive in connection with 'not'. The negation of a conjunction is a new tool, 'not both'.

On learning 'not' and 'and', the child already internalizes a bit of logic; for to affirm a compound of the form 'p and not p' is just to have mislearned one or both particles.

The child masters further connectives: 'above', 'beneath', 'before', 'after', 'in', 'beside', each of which serves to combine observation sentences two by two into a compound observation sentence. Perhaps the child learns such a connective by first learning a compound observation sentence outright as a whole by direct ostension. Then, having learned also each of the component sentences independently, he catches on to the trick and proceeds to apply the connective by analogy to other pairs.

One of these primitive grammatical constructions in particular is significant as a first step toward reification of bodies. Applied to the simple observation sentences 'Black' or 'That's black' and 'Dog' or 'That's a dog', it forms the compound 'Black dog', or 'The dog is black'. As an observation sentence the compound can be phrased either way, since terms are not yet recognized as denoting. I call this primitive grammatical construction *observational predication,* in anticipation of the mature predication into which it will evolve.

Although 'Black dog' and 'The dog is black' are not to be distinguished at this stage, observational predication is quite another matter from mere conjunction, 'Black and dog'. The conjunction describes any scene in which black and dog are both salient, whereas 'Black dog' requires that they be situated together, the black patch engulfing the canine patch. The predication expresses the compact clustering of visual qualities that is characteristic of a body.

Bodies are our first reifications: the first objects to be taken as objects. It is in analogy to them that all further positing of objects takes place. Surely they were the first for man as a talking species, and they are the first for the child. What sets them apart from other sources of stimulation? Typically a body contrasts with its visual surroundings in color and in movement or parallax, and typically it is fairly chunky and compact. If it is animate and seen full face, it is bilaterally symmetric. If we make contact, it resists pressure. It is merely such traits, at first, that distinguish bodies from the glow of the evening sky, the feel of a cool breeze, or other details of the passing show. The mode of compounding observation sentences that

I have called predication, then, is a step toward reification of bodies, in its stress on spatial clustering. However, I hold that at this point reification is not yet achieved. What more is required is a matter that I shall take up in the next chapter.

Meanwhile I turn to what I picture as the first step beyond ordinary observation sentences; namely a generalized expression of expectation. It is a way of joining two observation sentences to express the general expectation that whenever the one observation sentence holds, the other will be fulfilled as well. Examples: 'When it snows, it's cold'; 'Where there's smoke, there's fire'; 'When the sun rises, the birds sing'; 'When lightning, thunder'. They are our first faltering scientific laws. I call them *observation categoricals.*

In the evolution of language, and also in the child's learning of it, the leap from ordinary observation sentences to observation categoricals was a giant one. I would like to know how it came about and how it is learned. It was a vital development, for observation categoricals are the direct expression of inductive expectation, which underlies all learning.

The survival value of the apes' cries, and of our ordinary observation sentences, lay in vicarious observation: we learn about what only someone else can see from where he sits. Observation categoricals bring us much more. They bring us vicarious habituation, vicarious induction. One gets the benefit of generalized expectations built up over the years by some veteran observer or even by that veteran's own informant long dead. Observation categoricals can be handed down.

Even at this stage there is no denotation, no reference to bodies or other objects, to my way of reckoning. The observation categorical just asserts concomitance or close succession of separately specified phenomena. The child's observation sentences 'Mama' and 'Doggy' at this stage still merely register repeatable features of the passing show, on a par with 'Cold' and 'Thunder'. Any difference here is only qualitative, not ontological.

Even so, at this point naturalism's modest simulation of an old epistemological quest is achieved, in a primitive way. We have a sketch of a causal chain from the impacts of rays and particles on our receptors to a rudimentary theory of the external world. For the observation categoricals are indeed a theory of the world, complete with empirical checkpoints subject to the experimental method. An observation categorical is a miniature scientific theory that we can test experimentally by waiting for an occasion where the first component of the categorical is fulfilled, or even by bringing about its fulfillment, and then watching for fulfillment of the second component. An unfavorable outcome refutes the theory—the categorical. A favorable outcome leaves the theory for further consideration.

❧ III ❧

REIFICATION

WE HAVE NOW ARRIVED at a simulation of the most primitive phase of natural science. It achieves nothing, still, that I have deigned to recognize as reference to objects. What am I holding out for? Just the traditional sort of categorical: 'All ravens are black'. We can almost get it with the observation categorical 'Whenever there is a raven, there is a black raven'. But not quite. This categorical is compatible with albino ravens as long as they keep close company with black ones.

The crucial leap to reification of ravens can be achieved by just improving our near approximation by changing 'there' to 'it': 'Whenever there is a raven, *it* is a black raven'; 'Whenever there is a raven, it is black'; 'All ravens are black'.

The pronoun 'it' is a vital new link between the component observation sentences 'Raven' or 'Lo, a raven' and 'Black' or 'Lo, black'. It posits common carriers of the two traits, ravenhood and black. The carriers are ravens, bodies. I see this pronominal construction as achieving objective reference. An observation categorical of this strengthened sort, 'Whenever . . ., it . . .', I call a *focal* observation categorical. The earlier ones are *free* observation categoricals.

Reification can be seen as a leap from what Peter Geach calls pronouns of laziness (pp. 51–68) to essential pronouns. In the sentence 'I bumped my head and it hurts' the pronoun is one of laziness. It could be supplanted by its grammatical antecedent, 'my head': 'I bumped my head and my head hurts'. By contrast, in the focal categorical 'Whenever there is a raven, it is black' the pronoun is essential. Supplanting it by its grammatical antecedent, 'a raven', delivers only the weaker message 'Whenever there is a raven, a raven is black'. This is the free observation categorical again, compatible with white ravens. 'All ravens are black' requires the focal categorical, and hence the essential pronoun, and hence reification.

Multiple presentation—several ravens at a time—is at the bottom of it all. Multiple presentation itself can be taken in stride without all that, for we can learn 'Apple', 'Two apples', 'Three apples' each outright by direct ostension, and likewise 'Raven', 'Two ravens,' 'Three ravens', and then produce new cases by analogy. But multiple presentation of a black and a possibly albino raven is what made our free categorical fall short of 'All ravens are black'. Multiple presentation, again, is what calls for indefinite singular terms—'a raven', 'any raven', 'each raven', 'every raven', 'some raven'. Solitary presentations could be managed with 'the raven' or simply 'raven', on a par with 'thunder' or 'sunrise'. Indefinite singular terms, in turn, are the grammatical antecedents that call for essential pronouns.

I wonder, again, how this momentous move from free observation categorical to focal came about. Maybe it was just the happy neglect of the difference between essential pronouns and pronouns of laziness. I find this etiology amusing, in pinning the reification of bodies, the very dawn of the notion of object, on a confusion. We shall come to a further case of this sort. Happy confusions are frequent in biological evolution: a disused organ or accidental growth becomes diverted in a later generation, by natural selection, to a vital new use.

Boons, like people, are to be valued for themselves and not for their origins. Serendipity and opportunism are laws of nature.

Whatever its faltering origin, reification proved indispensable in connecting loose ends of raw experience to produce the beginnings of a structured system of the world. It is the advance from concomitances of disembodied phenomena such as 'Whenever lightning, thunder', or even 'Whenever raven, black raven', to generalized predication: 'All ravens are black'. Linguistically what is linking the loose ends of experience is the 'it' that links the two clauses.

One thinks of terms as our means of referring to objects. A definite singular term such as 'Taj Mahal' designates one object, ideally, and a general term or predicate denotes any number of them (Chapter VI). But C. S. Peirce placed primary responsibility for reference rather on the pronoun,[1] and such, we see, is my line.

Since the grammatical antecedents of essential pronouns are indefinite singular terms—'every raven', 'some raven'—we can gain logical economy by relegating the qualifying predicate, 'raven' here, to a component clause of the ensuing text. We can make do with just two indefinite singular terms: 'everything' (or 'everyone') and 'something' (or '-one'). 'Every raven is black' becomes 'Everything, if it is a raven, is black', and 'Some ravens are white' becomes 'Something is a raven and is white'. 'Everything' and 'something', finally, can be frozen into two fixed quantifiers: 'everything is such that' and 'something is such that'.

Ambiguity ensues, however. The trouble is familiar in ordinary English: 'Tom got Dick to paint his fence'. Whose fence? 'His' here is a pronoun of laziness, and we can resolve the

1. Volume 5, paragraph 153.

ambiguity by substituting the intended grammatical antecedent: 'Tom got Dick to paint Tom's (Dick's) fence'. In the case of an essential pronoun, however—'Someone got someone to paint his fence'—there is no such recourse. Nor is there after our proposed regimentation:

> Someone is such that someone is such that he got him to paint his fence.

This only makes matters worse. The likely recourse for either version is to 'former' and 'latter'. In other examples we need to resort to variables:

> Someone x is such that someone y is such that x got y to paint x's fence.

In symbols,

$$\exists x \exists y(x \text{ got } y \text{ to paint } x\text{'s fence}).$$

It was universal quantification, not existential, that we saw emerging in the focal observation categorical:

$$\forall x(x \text{ is a raven } .\supset. \ x \text{ is black}).$$

In extralogical practice, indeed, occasion for universal quantification scarcely arises except over a conditional or biconditional:

$$\forall x(Fx \supset Gx), \qquad \forall x(Fx \equiv Gx)$$

or, as Giuseppe Peano used to render them, '$Fx \supset_x Gx$' and '$Fx \equiv_x Gx$'. However, given that much, we can define the unrestricted quantification '$\forall Fx$' as '$(Fx \supset Fx) \supset_x Fx$'. Having

'$\forall xFx$', moreover, we can go on to define '$\exists xFx$' in familiar fashion as '$\sim\forall x \sim Fx$'.

Not that this is how existential quantification or its vernacular equivalent actually emerged, either in the race or in the child. But the interest in how it actually emerged dwindles when we see how in principle it could. Would that we could do as much for other crucial concepts.

There is a variant approach to quantification, reminiscent of Peano, that interlocks instructively with the concept of a predicate. It is a matter of seeing '$\exists xFx$' not as '$(\exists x)(Fx)$' but as '$\exists(x(Fx))$'; not as the application of a quantifier '$\exists x$' to an open sentence 'Fx', but as the application of '$\exists$' to a complex predicate 'xFx', 'x such that Fx'. Instead of reading '$\exists xFx$' as '(something x)(is such that Fx)', we take to reading it as '(something is)(x such that Fx)'.

Making this shift means recognizing an operator 'x such that' of *predicate abstraction,* in Peano's notation '$x\ni$', for encapsulating in a self-contained complex predicate all that a sentence affirms of an object. Just substitute 'x' for 'Tom' in the sentence, if Tom is the object in question, and prefix '$x\ni$' to the resulting open sentence. The complex predicate thus formed, when predicated of anyone, will say of him what the original sentence said of Tom. This is our familiar 'such that' idiom, which is mathematical pidgin English for our indigenous relative clause.

Parallel remarks apply to the universal quantifier: we can reconstrue '$\forall xFx$' as applying '$\forall$' to 'xFx', that is, to '$x\ni Fx$'. Our choice between the two attitudes to quantification is indifferent to its use and its logical laws, except that this variant way casts new light on our schematic letters 'F', 'G', etc. We always called them predicate letters anyway, but from this variant angle they become just that. Viewing '$\exists xFx$' and '$\forall xFx$' as '$\exists(xFx)$' and '$\forall(xFx)$' exposes the complex predicate 'xFx', or '$x\ni Fx$', which is precisely the predicate to view 'F' itself as standing for. The two occurrences of 'x' in '$x\ni Fx$' or 'xFx' thus cancel out, and we can simply write '$\forall F$' and '$\exists F$'.

The notation '$\exists F$', indeed, was Peano's own. His mature notation retains universal quantification only in the contexts '$Fx \supset_x Gx$' and '$Fx \equiv_x Gx$'. For simplicity and symmetry of logical theory, however, we are better off with '$\forall$', especially since '$\forall$' and '$\exists$' are interdefinable as '$\sim\exists\sim$' and '$\sim\forall\sim$'. An effect, moreover, is that variables become devices strictly and solely of predicate abstraction: '$x\ni$', 'x such that'. All other uses reduce to this. The variable comes to appear in its true light as purely a means of identifying and distinguishing the referential places in a sentence, and nothing to do with 'all' or 'some', which are the business of '$\forall$' and '$\exists$'. As for the etymology of 'variable', it should be studiously ignored; it rests on a pernicious old mathematical metaphor that is happily fading.

Predicate abstraction by 'such that', or its grammatically more complicated equivalent the English relative clause, confers *predicational completeness:* whatever we can say about a thing can be said about it by predicating a predicate of it. This is one more in the succession of epochs in the development of language, and again in the child's learning of it.

The appropriateness of linking reification to the essential pronoun, or to its counterpart the variable of quantification, is apparent to begin with from the vernacular paraphrases 'everything x' and 'something x' of the quantifiers. Another good perspective emerges when we see the basic role of the variable as the abstraction of predicates or, what are for me the same, general terms; for then the pertinent values of the variables are the things that fulfill the predicate, the things denoted by the general term. We are thus back to viewing terms as our means of referring to objects, but now it is not a question of being designated by a singular term; it is a question of being denoted by a general term. Most things are not individually specifiable by name or description; not practically, certainly, and in the case of irrational numbers, as Cantor proved, not even in principle. But all things are denoted by general terms, by 'thing', indeed, among others.

From either perspective, then, whether quantification or predicate abstraction, to be is to be a value of a variable. But this criterion of ontological commitment is parochial still, in that it applies directly only to theories constructed within the framework of our classical quantification theory, or predicate logic. Theories with access to other resources present a problem of foreign exchange. Failing translation into my adopted standard, I can only say that the word 'exists' has a different usage, if any, in that quarter. Given translation, on the other hand, the criterion simply carries over.

Such, then, is the cosmic burden borne by the humble variable. It is the locus of reification, hence of all ontology. Yet humble it is, since all use of it is reducible to its use in abstracting predicates from sentences. Here the variable serves merely to mark places where the same thing is referred to, and single it out as denoted by the newly abstracted predicate.

This clerical bit of permutation and recombination performed by the variable in its smoothly flowing way can be resolved into four *predicate functors:* four discrete operations comparable to simple arithmetic. Each applies to one predicate to produce another. One is '∃', which we have already been observing in operation on a one-place predicate, such as 'wombat', to produce a "no-place predicate," which is to say an outright sentence, 'there are wombats'. '∃' is generalized to apply to n-place predicates to produce $(n-1)$-place ones; thus '∃ loves' is a one-place predicate, the passive participle 'loved'.

$$(\exists F)x_2...x_n \equiv \exists x_1\ Fx_1...x_n.$$

I call the operation *cropping*. It pairs off with an unfamiliar *padding*, which turns n-place predicates into $(n + 1)$-place ones. Applied to 'dog', padding produces a two-place predicate that relates everything to every dog. In general,

$$(\text{Pad } F)x_0...x_n \equiv Fx_1...x_n.$$

A third operation, *reflection,* applies to two-place predicates to yield their reflexives: 'hate' goes into 'hate oneself'. More generally,

$$(\text{Refl } F)x_2...x_n \equiv Fx_2x_2x_3...x_n.$$

Finally there is a *permutation* functor 'Perm' that promotes the second argument of a many-place predicate to last place:

$$(\text{Perm } F)x_1x_3...x_nx_2 \equiv Fx_1...x_n.$$

These four functors do all the recombinatorial work of bound variables. When superimposed on the traditional Boolean algebra of sentences and predicates, couched in schematic letters 'F', 'G', ..., 'p', 'q', ... without variables, they afford a complete notation for predicate abstraction and indeed for the whole logic of truth functions and quantification. (See the appendix.)

The Boolean part is covered by two familiar predicate functors. One yields the *complement* '$-F^n$' where 'F^n' stands for an n-place predicate. The other yields the *intersection* 'F^nG^n' of the two predicates. '$-F^n$' denotes the sequences of length n not denoted by 'F^n', and 'F^nG^n' denotes those denoted jointly by 'F^n' and 'G^n'. Every schema of the logic of truth functions and quantification can be translated into one that is built up by applying our predicate functors, now six in number, to the schematic letters 'F', 'G', ...

The letters now have to bear exponents indicating how many places the represented predicates have, since there are no longer the appended strings of variables whose lengths answered that question. When we get down to 'F^o', 'G^o', . . ., we are down to no-place predicates, hence again to sentences. 'F^o', 'G^o' . . . stand in for the traditional 'p', 'q', ... '$-F^o$' and 'F^oG^o' are negation and conjunction.

Whatever the utility of predicate-functor logic to future computer technology, the variable is more congenial to the mind of man. The philosophical importance of the predicate functors is the resolution of the variable's magic into its pedestrian components, which are matters purely of order and recurrence of reference.

But now, absent the variable, what of reification? We have not lost it. In a predicate-functor culture, to be is to be denoted by a one-place predicate. This phrasing fits our home usage too, since any value of a variable is denoted by some predicate or other—indeed by '$x \ni (x = x)$'—and vice versa.

So much, then, for the logic of reification. Let us get back to cases. Long before reification in our clean-cut sense, bodies commanded the special attention of our remote ancestors, as they do that of modern man from early infancy. Natural selection had heightened man's responsiveness and that of other animals to the sight and smell of bodies, for there is survival value in prompt awareness of prey and predator. In the inchoate speech of early man and modern young children, bodies come to be hinted in the combining of observation sentences by observational predication (Chapter II). In the fullness of time we have the focal observation categorical, and eventually the relative clause or predicate abstraction. Our stock of predicates will meanwhile have grown with budding scientific theory, and now predicate abstraction offers us predicates for everything we can say about anything.

There is still a momentous further step of reification, wherever it may fit in the developmental sequence. It is the transcending of the specious present. Up to that point the reification of bodies is still sketchy, weak in the time dimension. There is as yet no sense in saying that this raven is the one we saw yesterday, or that it is not. We are still dealing with a stage of language that is limited to the specious present and to short-term memories and expectations. If at this stage of our development we recognize a particular body after a long absence, it is only by habituation to its distinctive observable traits. Distinguishing a body from an utterly similar one at a later time is what calls for the next big development. It requires acquisition of our whole schematism of space and time and the unobserved trajectories of bodies within it. A silver cup now viewed may be exactly similar to one viewed years ago without being the same one; and the original one may have tarnished and changed deceptively over the same period. Settling the question of identity would involve research and speculation about the movement of the cup or cups in our absence.

I picture our concepts of body, space, and time as evolving interdependently. To begin with, we recognize a recurrent body merely by strong perceptual similarity. Thus far, that particular recurrent body is on a par with cold, thunder, and other unitary repeatable features of the passing show. Next we distinguish fixed bodies from vagrant ones by the locomotive effort on our own part that accompanies the disappearance and recurrence of a fixed body. Fixed bodies then serve as tentative landmarks in a dawning conception of geography.

Perceptual similarity is disqualified early, as a sufficient condition of recurrence of one and the same body, by the spectacle
of two qualitatively indistinguishable apples side by side. Identity or distinctness over time, in the absence of qualitative differences, then becomes a matter rather of conjectural trajectories of objects between observations. Our science at length
progresses to where qualitative indistinguishability is neither
necessary nor sufficient for identity. A body can grow, shrink,
discolor.

The prehistoric breakthrough from the specious present into
the diachronic is imaginatively dramatized by Derek Bickerton:

Consider the following situation. You are Og. Your band has
just severely wounded a cave-bear. The cave-bear has with-
drawn into its cave. Ug wants to go after it. "Look blood.
Bear plenty blood. Bear weak. Ug go in. Ug kill bear. Ug
plenty strong." You want to be able to say something along
the lines of *the bear we tried to kill last winter had bled at
least as much as this one, but when Ig went in after it to finish
it, it killed him instead so don't be such an idiot.* Since in order
to think this all you had to be able to do was to replay the
memory of events you yourself had witnessed, I can see no
reason to believe that you could not have thought it because
you didn't have the words to think it in. But saying it is
another story. Let's suppose you try. Since you have nothing
approaching embedding, there is no way you can use a
relative clause to let the others know which bear you are
thinking about. Since you have no articles or any comparable
device, there is no way you can let the others know that you
are talking about a bear that they know about too. Since you
have no way of marking relative time by automatic tense
assignment or even adverbs, there is no way you can let the

others know that the bear you want to talk about is one that
is not here anymore. Since you have no verbs of psychologi-
cal action (we'll see why in a moment), there is no way you
can use the verb form itself to inform the others that you
are speaking of a past time (*remind, recall, remember,* etc.).
You can try "Og see other bear." Everybody panics. "Where?
Bear where?" "Bear not here." Some laugh, some get angry;
Og's up to his practical joking again. "Bear kill Ig," you try.
Now even the ones who are laughing are sneering. "Ig! Ig dead!
Og crazy!" If you have any sense, you shut up, or someone
will get the idea to push you into the cave instead of Ug.
(P. 270)

This breakthrough was such a boost to thought, Bickerton
speculates, that it may account for the emergence of agriculture
and towns nine millennia ago. He finds the same leap reen-
acted in modern times in the transition from pidgin to creole.
Pidgin is the faltering jargon that comes of the spontaneous
efforts of heterogeneous groups to communicate; creole is its
development in succeeding generations.

We can inquire more confidently into the ontogenetic as-
pect, tracing the modern child's progress from first observation
sentences to categoricals, logical particles, relative clauses, past
and future tense, and finally the diachronic individuation of
bodies. There is a substantial literature on the child's mental
and linguistic development, much of it from Jean Piaget's
group in Geneva around 1960 and much of it later. The data
recorded in these sources could perhaps be mined and re-
worked to account for the steps of development that are
concerning us here. Such an inquiry would no doubt suggest
further empirical studies directed at our present concerns.

Besides depending in general on conjectured trajectories and causal chains, moreover, the question of identity of a body from one time to another is generally meaningless apart from the choice of a governing predicate. Viewed four-dimensionally, a body is the content of a portion of space-time; and some portions of the body may qualify as bodies in turn. The tadpole is a body and the supervening four-legged frog is a different body, but together they make up a third body, a lifelong animal, a frog.

Failure to relativize sameness of object to kind of object has engendered bad philosophy. Am I the same person I was in my youth? or in my mother's womb? Will I be the same person after my brain transplant? These are not questions about the concept of identity, than which nothing could be more pellucid. They are questions about the concept of person, or the word 'person', which, like most words, goes vague in contexts where it has not been needed. When need does arise in hitherto unneeded contexts, we adopt a convention, or receive a disguised one from the Supreme Court.

Reification has continued beyond bodies and substances, adding new sorts of objects and new quantified conditionals to tighten the logical structure of science. Atoms tentatively entered the ontology already in antiquity, in easy analogy to the primordial bodies. Abstract objects were reified even earlier, it would seem, though there was nothing so suggestive in the way of analogy. Perhaps the first abstract objects to be assumed were properties, thanks again to a serendipitous confusion: a conflation again of essential pronouns with pronouns of laziness. Granted, the ancient Greeks were not speaking our language, but theirs was near enough.

Here is the scenario. A zoologist describes some peculiarity in the life-style of a strange invertebrate, and then adds, "It is true as well of the horseshoe crab." His 'it' is a pronoun of laziness, saving him the trouble of repeating himself. But let him and others conflate it with an essential pronoun, and we have them dreaming up a second-order predicate such as 'property' or 'attribute' to denote objects of a new kind, abstract ones, quantified over as values of variables.

Again a happy confusion, if confusion it was. Science would be hopelessly crippled without abstract objects. We quantify over them. In the harder sciences, numbers and other abstract objects bid fair to steal the show. Mathematics subsists on them, and serious hard science without serious mathematics is hard to imagine.

Even so, the pioneer abstract objects, which I take properties to have been, are *entia non grata* in my book. There is no entity without identity, and the identity of properties is ill defined. Properties are sometimes distinguished even though they are properties of entirely the same things; and there are no clear standards for so doing. However, the utility that made properties such a boon can be retained by deciding to equate properties that are true of all the same things, and to continue to exploit them under another name: classes.

Once the ice was broken, further abstract objects flooded in. Numbers, most conspicuously. Saying that there are nine planets does not yet reify the number nine, though in an explicitly regimented theory it may be seen to reify the class of planets. But we have reified numbers when we state laws of computation, or even ask whether nine is prime.

A physicalist ontology that is apparently adequate to all reality consists of just the physical objects, plus all classes of them, plus all classes of any of the foregoing, plus all classes of any of this whole accumulation, and so on up. Suitable versions of numbers, functions, and other mathematical objects get identified with denizens of this ontology, in the course of the glorious reduction of mathematics to logic and membership (Chapter I).

By way of ground elements, the physical objects, one thinks of integral masses of matter, notably bodies; but it is neither easy nor necessary to limit them thus. Better simply to admit as a physical object the content of any portion of space-time, however irregular, indeed however discontinuously scattered. Even my desk, after all, is discontinuous under hypermicroscopic magnification. An agreeable effect of this simplification is accommodation of substances, each as the single scattered designatum of a mass term: 'sugar', 'water'. Water, the one and only water, is the whole scattered aqueous portion of the spatiotemporal universe.

This lavishness of ground elements diminishes the need of classes. Biological taxonomy, seemingly the prime example of classes in natural science, can dispense with them altogether. Each taxon, be it a species or genus or family or phylum or whatever, can simply be identified with the spatiotemporally scattered physical object that contains as parts all the organisms belonging to it and that is exhausted by them. An organism is then a part, rather than a member, of its species; a species is a part, not a member, of its genus; and so on up. Parts of the organism are then likewise parts of the species and genus so construed. But *belonging* to a species is analyzed, under this approach, as being an organism *and* a part of the species. It is the overarching individuative predicate 'organism' that makes the reduction work.

It works thanks to the discreteness of organisms; no overlapping, no containment of one organism as part of another. It fails if we decide to count a fetus or mytochondrion both as an organism and as part of its host. Let's not.

It does not work for the states and counties of the United

States. On the one hand the class of all counties has some thirty-one hundred members, while the class of states has only fifty; on the other hand the aggregate physical object comprised of the counties—their *mereological* union or sum, so called—is indistinguishable from that of the states, being simply the United States itself, *e pluribus unum*. The reason we have to indulge in the abstraction of classes at all, at the level of classes of extended objects in space-time, is that some such objects overlap.

So it can happen that even a soft science requires classes, and even apart from any recognizable mathematics. The need is sometimes subtle, as illustrated by an example in which I am indebted to Peter Geach and David Kaplan: 'Some artists admire one another and no one else'. Kaplan proved that there is nothing for it but to assume at least one class of artists, each of whom admires the other members and no one else. But then hard science is waist deep in classical mathematics, which is set theory—class theory—from scratch.

֍ IV ֎

CHECKPOINTS AND EMPIRICAL CONTENT

ON THE HEELS of observation sentences we saw science emerging with the inception of observation categoricals. It had already begun with free observation categoricals (Chapter II), prior even to any reification. The categorical was a miniature scientific theory. Its antecedent clause was the experimental condition, and its consequent clause was the prediction.

Observation sentences, of which categoricals are compounded, change and develop as scientific knowledge grows. They develop down the years in the individual and down the centuries in society. Primitiveness is not what it takes to be an observation sentence. What it takes is two other traits, one private to the individual and the other public to society, as explained in Chapter II. The private requirement both early and late is just that the sentence be keyed directly to a range of perceptually fairly similar global stimuli, and not necessarily that it be learned by direct conditioning. An observation sentence can be acquired indirectly in later years through the intervention of sophisticated theory. A chemist learns about compounds of copper in the course of his reading and experiments, and a physician learns about the facial symptoms of an overactive thyroid; in due course the one comes to recognize the presence of copper by a glance at the solution, and the other to recognize hyperthyroidism by a glance at the patient. The sentence 'There was copper in it' has *become* an observation sentence for the one, and 'He's a hyperthyroid' for the other.

In the course of time the subject's early observation sentences, acquired by ostension, will themselves have changed at points, through continuing public pressure. He will perhaps no longer assent to 'Fish' on seeing a whale, as he once would have done.

As for the public requirement on observation sentences, namely unhesitating concurrence by all qualified witnesses, it comes to hinge increasingly on one or another narrowing of the pertinent linguistic community. Thus in two of our present examples the pertinent society is not all English speakers, but just chemists in one case and physicians in the other. The pertinent society, like the subject, becomes a parameter; an occasion sentence is an observation sentence with respect to a given individual and community, without counting as observational with respect to that individual and a wider community.

In all these respects the fund of observation categoricals will have evolved pari passu with their component clauses. Moreover, they are the lifeline of science; for I see them not just as miniature scientific theories individually, but as the ultimate empirical checkpoints of science generally. A theory is tested by deducing an observation categorical from it and testing the categorical. If it fails, so does the theory. One or another of its component assertions is false and needs to be retracted. If the categorical passes the test, then so far so good. A favorable test does not, of course, prove a theory to be true; it does not even prove the observation categorical to be true.

The social requirement on observation sentences plays two vital roles. First, it enables the child to learn the use of them from society. Second, it renders science objective, or anyway intersubjective. The narrowing of the pertinent community is a narrowing to the experimenter's trained colleagues. But the broad linguistic community retains philosophical relevance too in this context, for presumably the checking of a scientific hypothesis could in principle be tracked back to the layman's level by feigning doubt of each more sophisticated observation categorical and demanding more basic checks. It would be a matter of eliciting a résumé of antecedent experimental developments.

Note that in representing observation categoricals as the checkpoints of science I am close, after all, to the familiar line. The familiar line is that under appropriate observable conditions the theory that we are testing implies such and such observable results. I am merely combining the observable condition and observable result in a single sentence, a universal conditional, and calling upon the theory to imply the whole conditional. I thus simplify the logic.

We can tighten the account further by noting that the only categoricals that matter here are those that are *synthetic,* that is, not analytic. An observation categorical is *analytic* for a given speaker if the range of stimulations under which he is disposed to assent to the first of the two observation sentences in the categorical already includes all the stimulations under which he is disposed to assent to the second observation sentence, so that for him the categorical is trivially true out of hand and worthless in testing scientific hypotheses. I have long questioned the significance of the analytic-synthetic distinction when applied to theoretical sentences across the board, but I have here defined it as applied to observation categoricals.

Usually what calls for testing is a new hypothesis, concerning which the scientist is hopeful but open-minded. But usually it will not imply any synthetic observation categoricals outright.

What will do the implying is the hypothesis in conjunction with some background material, comprising sentences that the scientist already accepts as true.

But quite apart from new hypotheses the scientist may notice an interesting testable consequence of his current theory—hence an interesting observation categorical implied by his theory. He tests it and it fails, obliging him (ideally) to rescind some one or other from among those of his current tenets that combined to imply it. There are perhaps several on which the implication depended, and rescinding any one of them would resolve the problem. But the rescinding is no simple matter, for the scientist must also trace other tenets that, in combination, imply the one he is rescinding. Some of those must be rescinded too, to disempower *that* implication; and so on back.

Moreover, when there are several tenets each of which contributes thus to implying a given false observation categorical, the choice of which one to rescind is not immaterial. Rescinding any one would resolve *that* problem, yes; but different choices issue in different new theories, one of which would withstand future tests better than another. It is a spot where the good scientist is distinguished by his shrewd guess.

The simple schematism of observation categoricals and implication is remote from the experimental scientist's overt or conscious practice. For logical implication to hold, we must admit among the premises various self-evident truths and familiar laws of nature that the scientist takes in stride quite unconsciously. Moreover the relation of implication will be for the scientist just a matter of "standing to reason"; he seeks bigger game than logical minutiae. Also there may be some brief backtracking along the way. A rough physical generalization in the *ceteris paribus* vein may have figured among the premises that implied a false categorical, so he will go back to that generalization and canvass the pertinent *cetera* for one that was not *par*. Having found and adjusted it, he will experiment again.

Moreover, there is some ongoing input of information from the outside world that is not limited to the specious present and hence is not directly accessible to observation sentences. It is conveyed neither through the five senses nor by kinesthesis in the manner of our awareness of walking uphill. I think of internal discomfort or other delayed effects of something we ate or drank. Such data do not go into observation sentences, for failure of intersubjectivity; but they are still grist for the mill of science. They are caught by observation sentences that report the patient's current manifestations, verbal and otherwise, of discomfort. An antecedently developed scientific theory links these manifestations both to their present presumed cause, dyspepsia, and to the remoter causes that were indeed intersubjectively observable the night before. Even these latter are no longer observable, but they are known through current testimony, from the patient or other witnesses, regarding the night before. The causal links between current observable testimony and the past events testified to are again part of the network of scientific theory.

It might be worthwhile to elicit the checkpoints of some substantial fragment of science, say Newtonian mechanics, by reconstructing all the myriad tacit logical steps and platitudes and formulating adequate observation categoricals, hence plausible corroboratory experiments, across the board. Such a study, if successful, would prompt others of the kind and perhaps contribute to the advancement of natural science by uncovering unexpected logical interconnections and suggesting a fruitful new hypothesis for testing.

It has been held by "positivists" of one or another stripe over the past century or two that a closed sentence is meaningless unless it has *empirical content*—exception being made perhaps for mathematics. The schematism of observation categoricals affords, it would seem, the standard of having empirical content. A set of sentences that has *critical mass,* as we may say—that is, that implies some synthetic observation categoricals—may be said to have those categoricals as its empirical content.

We have now accounted for empirical content for a sentence or set of sentences with critical mass, but what of other sentences? A sentence without critical mass might be felt still to have empirical content in a participatory way if it is a supporting member of a set with critical mass; that is, if its withdrawal deprives the set of empirical content.

However, this is fallacious. Any sentence, even Russell's 'Quadruplicity drinks procrastination', is a supporting member of a set that implies an observation categorical. Let us abbreviate Russell's sentence as 'q', and some observation categorical as 'c'. The two-member set $\{ {}'q', {}'q \supset c'\}$ implies 'c', but the one-member set $\{ {}'q \supset c'\}$ does not. So Russell's sentence is a supporting member of $\{ {}'q', {}'q \supset c'\}$. The same trick is readily embedded in less trivial examples.

The sentences we would like to credit with empirical content are ones that are supporting members of *interesting* sets with critical mass, sets that are not only testable but worth testing; hence sets whose members either are adjudged true or are up for consideration, unlike '$q \supset c$'. I see no way of molding this requirement into a rigorous standard of shared content. The really clear notion of having content is just critical mass. Some single sentences have it, most do not.

Even if I had a satisfactory notion of shared content, I would not want to impose it in a positivist spirit as a condition of meaningfulness. Much that is accepted as true or plausible even in the hard sciences, I expect, is accepted without thought of its joining forces with other plausible hypotheses to form a testable set. Such acceptations may be prompted by symmetries and analogies, or as welcome unifying links in the structure of the theory. Surely it often happens that a hypothesis remote from all checkpoints suggests further hypotheses that are testable. This must be a major source of hypotheses worth testing. Positivistic insistence on empirical content could, if heeded, impede the progress of science.

In softer sciences, from psychology and economics through sociology to history (I use 'science' broadly), checkpoints are sparser and sparser, to the point where their absence becomes rather the rule than the exception. Having reasonable grounds is one thing, and implying an observation categorical is another. Observation categoricals are implicit still in the predicting of archaeological finds and the deciphering of inscriptions, but the glories of history would be lost if we stopped and stayed at the checkpoints.

A normative domain within epistemology survives the conversion to naturalism, contrary to widespread belief, and it is concerned with the art of guessing, or framing hypotheses. The most general of its norms are perhaps conservatism, or the maxim of minimum mutilation, and simplicity, familiar in ontological contexts as Ockham's razor. No general calibration of either conservatism or simplicity is known, much less any comparative scale of the one against the other. For this reason alone—and it is not alone—there is no hope of a mechanical procedure for optimum hypothesizing. Creating good hypotheses is an imaginative art, not a science. It is the art of science.

Normative epistemology is the art or technology not only

of science, in the austere sense of the word, but of rational belief generally. Literature has burgeoned in this domain, and I do not see how the shift from phenomenalism to naturalism would conflict with it. Podiatry, appendectomy, and the surgical repair of hernias are technological correctives of bad side effects of natural selection, and such also in essence is normative epistemology in its correcting and refining of our innate propensities to expectation by induction. A vest-pocket specimen of this is the exposure and correction of the gambler's fallacy: the insidious notion that a run of bad luck increases the likelihood that the next try will win.

Correction of this sort of error is the therapeutic side of statistical theory, a substantial branch of applied mathematics that is part and parcel of normative epistemology. The central concern of statistical theory is probability, and subjective probability is degree of belief. The recent study of subjective probability by Brian Skyrms and Karel Lambert has an explicitly epistemological orientation. Other studies of it, pursuant on the work of Frank P. Ramsey in the 1920s, grade off into the thriving field of decision theory, which has in part congealed into John von Neumann and Oskar Morgenstern's austerely mathematical discipline of game theory. Studies in decision theory by Donald Davidson and Richard Jeffrey reveal a remarkable interlocking of subjective probability with the subject's preferences on one hand and the interpretation of his sentences on the other. Davidson's semantic program of interpretation involves playing each of these three variables—probability, preference, and interpretation—against the other two.

❦ V ❧

LOGIC AND MATHEMATICS

IMPLICATION, we have seen, is the lifeblood of theories, or perhaps better the finger of their fate. It is what relates a theory to its checkpoints in observation categoricals. What defines implication? Elementary predicate logic is enough: the truth functions and quantification. As hinted in Chapter II, the basic laws of logic in this sense are internalized in childhood, in acquiring the use of the logical particles 'not', 'and', 'or', 'some', 'every'. In our mathematical maturity we can encapsulate this logic in a complete formalization describable from scratch in a couple of pages. More briefly still, for those abreast of the jargon, it is as follows. To prove that a given set of premises implies a contemplated conclusion, prove that the premises are inconsistent with the negation of that conclusion. Do so by putting the premises and the negated conclusion into prenex form and then accumulating a truth functional inconsistency by persistent instantiation of the universal and existential quantifiers, taking care to use a new variable for each existential instantiation.[1]

Implication thus defined is all we need to mean by implica-

---

1. For a more elementary exposition see my *Methods of Logic*, 4th ed., pp. 190–193, 205–206.

tion. The laws of set theory and the rest of mathematics can be ranged rather among the premises that are doing the implying, on a par with the laws and hypotheses of natural science.

I like to limit the term 'logic' thus narrowly and to treat set theory as another, higher branch of mathematics. The contrasts between the two domains are profound. One difference is that logic so construed, unlike set theory, has no objects it can call its own; its variables admit all values indiscriminately. Another difference is that logic has no predicates and hence no sentences it can call its own, unless we count the identity predicate as logical.

This we may indeed choose to do, for identity is marginal in a curious way. Namely, any theory with any finite number of other primitive predicates gets identity too as a bonus. For identity can be defined, or something to the same formal purpose, by exhaustion of those primitive predicates. For example, if the primitive predicates are 'P', 'Q', and a dyadic 'R', we can define '$x = y$' as

$$\forall z(Px \equiv Py . Qx \equiv Qy . Rxz \equiv Ryz . Rzx \equiv Rzy).$$

A third difference between logic and set theory is that logic as I am construing it, with or without identity, admits of complete proof procedures. This was demonstrated by Gödel in 1930. I presented one such complete procedure four paragraphs back, and it is easily extended to identity. But from Gödel's great incompleteness theorem of 1931 it follows that set theory, even the mere theory of sets of individuals, admits of no complete proof procedure. In this regard it is like most branches of mathematics.

Hence my stress on the difference between logic, narrowly construed, and the rest of mathematics, including set theory. However, I am inclined to lighten somewhat the emphatic contrast usually drawn between mathematics and natural science. I already equated the roles of mathematical laws and laws of nature in the implying of observation categoricals. Let us reflect now on what *does* distinguish mathematics from natural science.

The accepted wisdom is that mathematics lacks empirical content. This is not contradicted by the participation of mathematics in implying the categoricals, for we saw (Chapter IV) that such participation does not confer empirical content. The content belongs to the implying set, and is unshared by its members. I do, then, accept the accepted wisdom. No mathematical sentence has empirical content, nor does any set of them. No conjunction or class of purely mathematical truths, however large, could ever imply a synthetic observation categorical. It seems obvious, and I accept it (though I can't picture how a proof would look). Every critically massive set of truths has some nonmathematical members.

This trait is not, however, peculiar to mathematics. There is no end of other equally infinite classes of truths, though less homogeneous than the class of mathematical truths, of which we can say that the whole infinite class, like mathematics, lacks empirical content. It is just a matter of malicious mixing. Any random handful of scientific truths is likely to fail to imply any synthetic observation categoricals. Amassing any number of such sterile sets, then, and taking care to avoid any cross-fertility between them, we can surely amass a class of truths of natural science without limit of size and without empirical content. What is interesting about mathematics in this regard is just that the mathematical truths, unlike the imagined miscellaneous assemblage, are somehow all of a kind. Somehow? How?

What obtrude as distinctly mathematical are various of what Tarski called *formalized languages.* Such a language comprises the sentences built from a fixed finite lot of basic predicates by predication, truth functions, and quantification—or, equivalently, by predicate functors. One such language is that of elementary number theory. Its basic predicates may be viewed as just two in number: the three-place predicates 'Σ' and 'Π' of addition and multiplication. 'Σxyz' means that $x = y + z$ and 'Πxyz' means that $x = y \cdot z$. We can proceed to define '$x = y$' as

$$\forall z(\Sigma zxx \equiv \Sigma zyy).$$

Then, with the help of identity, we can define the notation '$\imath x$ Fx' of singular description in Russell's familiar contextual way, and thus recover the familiar arithmetical notations

$$y + z = \imath x\, \Sigma xyz, \qquad 1 = \imath x\, (\Pi xxx \,.\, {\sim}\Sigma xxx),$$
$$y \cdot z = \imath x\, \Pi xyz, \qquad 2 = 1 + 1,$$
$$0 = \imath x\, \Sigma xxx, \qquad 3 = 2 + 1.$$

By defining 'Σ' and 'Π' in terms of 'ϵ' in any of the known ways, we can embed this closed language in the formalized language whose sole predicate is 'ϵ' itself, and which embraces all of classical mathematics (Chapter I). But there are also of course countless formalized languages foreign to classical mathematics. A trivial example is that of kinship, whose predicates are the one-place predicate 'F' ('female') and the two-place predicate 'P' ('parent'). We can express 'x is male' as '${\sim}Fx$', 'x is half or full sibling of y' as '$\exists z(Pzx \,.\, Pzy)$', 'x is mate of y' (roughly) as '$\exists z(Pxz \,.\, x \neq y \,.\, Pyz)$', and on to uncle, grandfather, third cousin twice removed. Typical truths in this language are the symmetry of sibling, mate, and cousin, the asymmetry of parent, and the transitivity of full sibling. Though foreign to classical mathematics, kinship theory smacks distinctively of mathematics in its trivial way, and I do not hesitate so to classify it.

The mere notion of a formalized language cannot, however, be said to capture the essence of mathematics. What perhaps induces mathematical flavor is paucity of primitive predicates, with consequent stress on logical construction. Mathematicity is perhaps a matter of degree. At any rate I have no demarcation to propose. The fact that the variables of classical mathematics take abstract objects as values while those of kinship take people or other animals is not a significant difference. Indeed 'ϵ' itself battens on concrete objects as first argument.

If we release geometry from the Procrustean bed of abstract relation theory and restore it to its pristine state as of Euclid's day, it falls outside the formalized language of 'ϵ' and becomes a formalized language on its own, a substantial and venerable analogue of my trivial kinship theory. Its predicates revert to denoting surfaces, curves, and points in real space. Like kinship theory, geometry is mathematics with an emphatically empirical subject matter. What eventually banished it to the limbo of uninterpreted mathematics was the logical anomaly of Euclid's postulate of parallels: its resistance to deduction from his simpler postulates. This stimulated exploration of alternative postulates, those of the non-Euclidean geometries, and exploration eventually of the limitless domain of uninterpreted systems, abstract algebras.

If Euclidean geometry still retained its old status of mathematics with a subject matter, it lost it when Einstein established that space itself, as defined by the paths of light, is non-Euclidean. In general, moreover, quite apart from geometry, disinterpretation came to play an indispensable role in proof theory. An effect may have been to exaggerate whatever cleavage may have been sensed between mathematics and the rest of science.

Uninterpreted mathematics is of course devoid not only of empirical content but of all question of truth and falsity. As for the theory that treats of those uninterpreted systems, hence of abstract algebras, it is part of the theory of relations and hence is interpreted mathematics, covered by set theory.

A word finally about the higher reaches of set theory itself and kindred domains which there is no thought or hope of applying in natural science. When I likened mathematical truths to empirical ones on the score of their helping to imply observation categoricals, I was disregarding these mathematical flights. As empiricists, how should we view them?

They are couched in the same vocabulary and grammar as applicable mathematics, so we cannot simply dismiss them as gibberish, unless by imposing an absurdly awkward gerrymandering of our grammar. Tolerating them, then, we are faced with the question of their truth and falsehood. Many of these sentences can be dealt with by the laws that hold for applicable mathematics. Cases arise, however (notably the axiom of choice and the continuum hypothesis), that are demonstrably independent of prior theory. It seems natural at this point to follow the same maxim that natural scientists habitually follow in framing new hypotheses, namely, simplicity: economy of structure and ontology.

The strictures of economy are no threat to the starry-eyed set theorist for whom the sky is the limit. They do not declare any of his sentences meaningless; they merely slant our distribution of truth values so as to favor economy.[2] His tracing of implications among them still makes proof-theoretic sense and can be methodologically illuminating as well as exhilarating.

Regardless of predilections for economy or abundance, however, we know from Gödel's incompleteness theorem that every consistent proof procedure is bound to leave infinitely many

2. See my *Selected Logic Papers,* 2d ed., p. 243.

closed sentences of classical mathematics indemonstrable and irrefutable. A stronger proof procedure will catch more of them, but never all. Nor can we banish the outliers, even by acquiescing in a heroically complex gerrymandering of grammar; for there is no way in general of knowing which ones they are. Should we declare them meaningful but neither true nor false? This only puts a name to the predicament while complicating the logic.

I see nothing for it but to make our peace with the situation. We may simply concede that every statement in our language is true or false, but recognize that in these cases the choice between truth and falsity is indifferent both to our working conceptual apparatus and to nature as reflected in observation categoricals. It is like Kant's thing in itself, but seen as a matter of human usage rather than cosmic mystery.

There is a parallel in our accommodation of vagueness, if we shun the accommodations proposed in latter-day "fuzzy logic." What I call my desk could be equated indifferently with countless almost coextensive aggregates of molecules, but I refer to it as a unique one of them, and I do not and cannot care which. Our standard logic takes this also in stride, imposing a tacit fiction of unique though unspecifiable reference.

DENOTATION AND TRUTH

SEMANTICS IS CONCERNED with linguistic expressions in two respects: reference and meaning. Reference by a singular term is *designation;* 'Boston' designates Boston. Reference by a general term or predicate is *denotation;* 'rabbit' denotes each rabbit. Meaning is neither. The singular terms 'metropolis of New England' and 'capital of Massachusetts' designate the same thing, namely Boston, but differ in meaning. The predicates 'born with a heart' and 'born with kidneys' denote the same individuals, I am told, but they differ in meaning.

Meaning is for the next chapter. As for denotation and designation, denotation is where the action is. It takes designation in stride, for a singular term can be recast as a predicate that happens to denote just one thing if any. The singular term 'Boston', *designating* Boston, can be reconstrued as a predicate 'is Boston', *denoting* only Boston. Anything said about Boston can be paraphrased using 'is Boston'. 'Poe was from Boston' becomes

$$\exists x(x \text{ is Boston . Poe was from } x)$$

or, equally,

$$\forall x(x \text{ is Boston . } \supset \text{ . Poe was from } x).$$

We can settle for this as an economical foundation and still derive our usual and more convenient idiom of singular terms by singular description:

$$\text{Boston} = \imath x(x \text{ is Boston}).$$

Functors such as 'plus' and 'times', which generate complex singular terms, can be accommodated similarly, as illustrated in Chapter V by 'Σ' and 'Π'. The convenience of singular terms, however, is indispensable in practice. Mathematics would be paralyzed without the direct substitution of singular terms for variables and of equals for equals.

For what follows we must come squarely to terms with 'denote'. Since it is often used interchangeably with 'designate', and a singular term normally designates one and only one object, readers are apt to think of denotation as relating a predicate likewise to a single object, namely the class of all the things it is true of, or a property shared by them. In my use of 'denote', as in John Stuart Mill's,[1] a predicate denotes rather each separate thing of which it is true. The class or property is not involved.

For years, to obviate confusion, I avoided 'denote' altogether in favor of 'true of'; but that evasion would be impracticable in these pages, where denotation is becoming the center of action. Unlike Mill, I still withhold the word from singular terms; they are well served by 'designate'.

A word of caution is in order regarding 'predicate' too. Some logicians take a predicate as a *way* of building a sentence around a singular term or, more concretely, as what Peirce called a *rheme*,[2] a sentence with blanks in it, these being distinctively marked in the case of a many-place predicate. This version

1. Mill, Chapter II, §5.
2. Volume 2, paragraph 95.

covers, implicitly, the potential output of predicate abstraction or predicate functors. But a predicate in my sense is always an integral word, phrase, or clause, grammatically a noun, adjective, or verb. Some are generated from others by grammatical constructions, notably the relative clause or, formally, predicate abstraction or predicate functors.

Denotation, explained thus far only for one-place predicates, is needed also for predicates of two and more places. Two-place predicates, such as transitive verbs, may be said to denote ordered pairs, and n-place predicates denote sequences of length n.

An ordered pair $\langle x, y \rangle$ differs from a two-membered class $\{x, y\}$ in that the pair must determine x uniquely and y uniquely. That is,

$$(1) \qquad \langle x, y \rangle = \langle z, w \rangle \; .\equiv. \; x = z \, . \, y = w.$$

This is the sole requirement, and there are various artificial ways of construing ordered pairs as classes, all meeting the requirement. The usual way, due to Norbert Wiener in 1914 with subsequent modification by Kazimierz Kuratowski, is to identify $\langle x, y \rangle$ with the class $\{\{x\}, \{x, y\}\}$ whose members are the unit class $\{x\}$ of x and the class $\{x, y\}$ of x and y. A little reflection shows that it determines x uniquely as the member of every member of $\langle x, y \rangle$, and y as the other member of a member of $\langle x, y \rangle$ if such there be, and otherwise as x.

The two-place predicate 'father (of)', then, denotes $\langle$James Mill, John Stuart Mill$\rangle$, and 'son (of)' denotes $\langle$John Stuart Mill, James Mill$\rangle$. For denotation by predicates of three places and more, we need sequences of length three and longer. These can be defined by iteration of the pair, thus:

$$\langle x, y, z \rangle = \langle\langle x, y \rangle, z \rangle, \qquad \langle x, y, z, w \rangle = \langle\langle x, y, z \rangle, w \rangle,$$

and so forth.

Unbridled denotation, however, even by one-place predicates, is prey to paradox, as Kurt Grelling showed in 1908. The predicate 'not denoting self', or in a word 'heterologous', is where paradox strikes. The predicate 'English' is itself English, and 'short' is short; they denote themselves. 'German' and 'long' do not, and are thus heterologous. Most predicates are heterologous. But the predicate 'heterologous' itself, in particular, qualifies as heterologous if and only if it does not. Such is the paradox.

Structurally it is of a piece with Russell's familiar and devastating paradox, which he communicated to Frege in 1902: the paradox of the class of all classes not members of themselves. That one was what imposed limits on the reification of classes, by showing that not all predicates, or open sentences in one variable, can determine classes. Nor could the inconsistent cases be rounded up one by one and banished; for it turned out that countless further cases are self-consistent one by one but jointly incompatible. The result was the multiplicity of axiomatic set theories we know today, each with its peculiar claims to interest but incompatible with one another.

The special significance of Grelling's paradox, for all its kinship to Russell's, is that it is not rooted in reification and so cannot be uprooted by rescinding untenable reifications. It shows that the very word 'heterologous' must be to blame, despite its clear definition as 'not denoting self'. The finger of blame moves to this triad of words, and comes to rest on 'denoting'.

We have said little in definition or explication of the predicate 'denote', but evidently enough to plunge it into self-contradiction. The only condition we imposed was the *disquotation* paradigm: 'rabbit' denotes a thing if and only if the thing is a rabbit. It is disquotation, and it alone, that makes the predicate 'not denoting self' denote itself if and only if it does not. For all its seeming modesty, the disquotation requirement is too immodest for complete fulfillment.

What then of a *consistent* version of denotation? In 1935 Alfred Tarski solved the problem for formalized languages.[3] First we define denotation for each of the finitely many primitive predicates of the language, by disquotation. Thus, where 'F' stands for an n-place predicate,

$$\text{`}F\text{' denotes } \langle x_1, \ldots, x_n \rangle \, . \equiv Fx_1 \ldots x_n.$$

For derived predicates, then, we turn to the predicate functors (Chapter III). Thus,

$$\text{`}-F\text{' denotes } \langle x_1, \ldots, x_n \rangle \, . \equiv$$
$$\sim (\text{`}F\text{' denotes } \langle x_1, \ldots, x_n \rangle),$$

$$\text{`}F \cap G\text{' denotes } \langle x_1, \ldots, x_n \rangle \, . \equiv .$$
$$\text{`}F\text{' denotes } \langle x_1, \ldots, x_n \rangle \, . \, \text{`}G\text{' denotes } \langle x_1, \ldots, x_n \rangle,$$

$$\text{`}\exists F\text{' denotes } \langle x_2, \ldots, x_n \rangle \, . \equiv$$
$$\exists x_1 (\text{`}F\text{' denotes } \langle x_1, \ldots, x_n \rangle),$$

$$\text{`Pad } F\text{' denotes } \langle x_0, \ldots, x_n \rangle \, . \equiv .$$
$$\text{`}F\text{' denotes } \langle x_1, \ldots, x_n \rangle,$$

$$\text{`Refl } F\text{' denotes } \langle x_2, \ldots, x_n \rangle \, . \equiv .$$
$$\text{`}F\text{' denotes } \langle x_2, x_2, x_3, \ldots, x_n \rangle,$$

$$\text{`Perm } F\text{' denotes } \langle x_1, x_3, \ldots, x_n, x_2 \rangle \, . \equiv .$$
$$\text{`}F\text{' denotes } \langle x_1, \ldots, x_n \rangle.$$

This constitutes an inductive definition of denotation on the part of all predicates, primitive and definable, of the formalized language in question.

Denotation so defined does indeed obey disquotation, but our

3. Where I treat of denotation of sequences by predicates, Tarski treated of satisfaction of open sentences by sequences of values of their free variables. But it comes to the same thing.

inductive definition only explains denotation on the part of predicates constructible from the basic ones by predicate functors—hence by truth functions and quantification. Grelling's paradox assures us that 'denote' itself is not among these, or anyway warns us that it better not be.

So our inductive definition of denotation is incomplete, failing to define denotation on the part of the two-place predicate 'denote' itself and other predicates constructible from it. We can cover this further ground by repeating our whole inductive definition, but now treating our newly defined 'denote' as one of the basic predicates, labelled 'denote$_1$'. In this way we define 'denote$_2$'. It proves disquotational in application to all the basic predicates and to 'denote$_1$' and to all predicates constructible from all these by predicate functors (or by truth functions and quantification). We can then go on to 'denote$_3$' and so on up. For purposes other than studies of the present sort, however, denotation$_1$ is sufficient and can do without the subscript.

The inductive definition of denotation and its hierarchic implications, due essentially to Tarski, are relative to a formalized language and hence to some definite glossary of basic predicates. In ordinary practice, even when regimented in predicate logic, there is no such glossary, no fixed distinction between what is basic and what derivative, what is primitive and what defined. Consequently the construction does not apply directly to actual science and daily affairs. Still, Grelling's paradox does apply there. The relevance of our present construction to science and daily affairs, then, is to reveal the roots of the paradox and how to extirpate them. The lessons are that denotation comes in levels and that a denotation predicate of any one level cannot be trusted to operate in normal disquotational fashion when applied to another denotation predicate unless the latter is of lower level. The significance of the construction for actual language is that it gives the rationale for the hierarchy.

Denotation, then, stretches in two dimensions. There is the vertical dimension of hierarchy, and there is the horizontal dimension of length of denoted sequences: an n-place predicate denotes sequences of length n. Extrapolation, the mathematician's patellar reflex, prompts a question regarding this horizontal dimension: What about zero? What might qualify as a no-place predicate? We settled that in Chapter III. It is simply a closed sentence.

What then of denotation, in this degenerate case? In other cases, an n-place predicate denoted a given n-place sequence if and only if it was true of it. In the zero case, there being nothing for the no-place predicate to be true *of,* denotation reduces simply to truth outright. The zero case of denotation by predicates is truth of sentences. Truth, one might risk being quoted as saying, is just a degenerate case of denotation.

Truth falls in with the rest of the family in respect of disquotation. Just as

'Between' denotes $\langle x, y, z \rangle$.$\equiv$. x is between y and z,
'Father' denotes $\langle x, y \rangle$.$\equiv$. x is father of y,
'Rabbit' denotes x .$\equiv$. x is a rabbit,

so

'Snow is white' is true .$\equiv$. snow is white.

This last biconditional is the familiar trademark of Tarski's study of truth.

All predicates definable from the primitive ones by truth functions and quantification are forthcoming through the predicate functors, and so in particular are the no-place predicates, or closed sentences. Where 'F^0' stands for any such, then, and our object language is couched in predicate functors, we can define truth of 'F^0' in terms of denotation by the one-place predicate 'Pad F^0':

$$'F^0' \text{ is true } . \equiv \forall x('\text{Pad } F^0' \text{ denotes } x)$$
$$(\equiv \exists x('\text{Pad } F^0' \text{ denotes } x)).$$

Truth shares the infirmity of the rest of the denotation family: the susceptibility to paradox. Truth indeed is where it all began, in antiquity: the paradox of the liar, 'I am lying', or 'This sentence is false'. The demonstrative 'This' here is perhaps unpersuasive, for it simply recurs when we try to redeem it by substituting the designated sentence. However, we can dodge it by a resort to *self-predication* reminiscent of Grelling's paradox. The self-predication of an open sentence in one free variable is what we get by taking that open sentence itself as the value of its variable. Thus the self predication of the open sentence

The self-predication of x is false

is the closed sentence

The self-predication of 'The self-predication of x is false' is false.

But this is a paradox, predicating falsity of itself. Truth, like all denotation, must retreat up the hierarchy. At each level truth is simply denotation by no-place predicates, or sentences.

Disquotation has lent truth an air of triviality. Ramsey called disquotation the disappearance theory of truth, evidently underestimating the power of quotation. Far from triviality, disquotation determines truth uniquely. If two predicates 'true' and 'True' both fulfill disquotation, they are coextensive; for, where 'p' stands for a sentence,

$$\text{'}p\text{' is true } .\equiv p \equiv. \text{ '}p\text{' is True.}$$

Disquotation even determines truth more than uniquely, we saw, plunging it into paradox.

Along with this seriocomic blend of triviality and paradox, truth is felt to harbor something of the sublime. Its pursuit is a noble pursuit, and unending. In viewing truth thus we are viewing it as a single elusive goal or grail. In sober fact the pursuit resolves into concern with particular sentences, ones important to us in one or another way. Some truths are elusive, some not; some worth pursuing, some not. Thanks to the negation sign, there are as many truths as falsehoods; we just can't always be sure which are which.

Pursuit of truth is implicit, still, in our use of 'true'. We should and do currently accept the firmest scientific conclusions as true, but when one of these is dislodged by further research we do not say that it had been true but became false. We say that to our surprise it was not true after all. Science is seen as pursuing and discovering truth rather than as decreeing it. Such is the idiom of realism, and it is integral to the semantics of the predicate 'true'. It fittingly vivifies scientific method, the method of interrogating nature by conjecture and experiment and abiding by the consequences.

❧ VII ❧

SEMANTIC AGREEMENT

IN CHAPTER III we saw reification at work forging sameness of reference between clauses. That is what it is for. The function of identity is recurrence in discourse. Reification began by forging joint reference on the part of the clauses of a focal observation categorical. Next it joined forces with the budding schematism of space and time, to forge the identity of an object from one place and time to another. Here the contribution was reciprocal: recurrences of enduring bodies linked up the place-times as well as vice versa.

But there is still one question of sameness of reference. Besides sameness of reference in the two clauses of a focal observation categorical and sameness of reference across time, there is intersubjective sameness. Bodies present no evident problem here; intersubjective agreement is established in primary cases by ostension, nearly enough, and indirectly in other cases by reduction to those primary cases through causal chains established or conjectured in our growing science. I shall come back to this.

When we come to abstract objects, however, there is no such recourse. Who is to say whether what you refer to as the number nine is the same thing as what I refer to by that phrase? We both say that it is the size of the class of the planets, but who is to say that your two-place predicate 'size of' relates the same things as mine does? For that matter, there is no saying whether your class of the planets is the same as mine, even granted that we agree on each planet. Your class of the planets has the same members, in your sense of 'member', as mine does in my sense of 'member', but there the matter is left hanging. I submit that intersubjective sameness of reference makes no sense, as applied to abstract objects, beyond what is reflected in successful dialogue.

Much the same is true even of concrete objects when we move beyond the reach of ostension and consider theoretical objects such as elementary particles. To revive an old example of mine, picture two physicists pondering a crisis in particle physics. Each of them proposes a new particle. One proposes a particle without rest mass, and the other a particle with rest mass. Both of them apply the same new word, 'neutrino'. Query: are they disagreeing about the mass of the same particles, or are they positing different particles under the same name? Clearly it is an empty question.

Regarding gross bodies, I remarked above that intersubjective sameness presents no *evident* problem; also that I would come back. Consider now the scientific philosopher who is seeking a close-knit and economical system of the world. He identifies bodies with the portions of space-time that they occupy. He deals similarly with substances and with portions of substances. Sensible qualities of the bodies and substances simply carry over to these four-dimensional regions. A body is now a sinuous filament of space-time, long perhaps in the time dimension, colorful to the eye and resistant to the touch. We would say not that bodies have given way to space-time, but that they have been identified with or interpreted as space-time.

Still no problem. Next, however, our philosopher identifies

a point of space-time with the quadruple of numbers that are its coordinates in some arbitrary frame of reference. It is a matter of economy, since he needs the numbers in his science anyway. A body then becomes a class of quadruples of numbers—what I shall call a *number table*. So likewise for any substance, however scattered and diffuse. Our sensory associations now carry over to these abstract number tables.

This still need not be thought of as an extravagant reinterpretation of terms that formerly denoted familiar things. We learned names and predicates for the things by ostension and can continue to do so. As always, the pointing just serves to enhance the salience of the features of our sensory input that are to be associated with the object, albeit a number table. We need not know any numbers.

This example came of two steps that we can suppose are motivated by considerations of ontological economy: identification of physical objects with spatiotemporal regions and identification of these with number tables. However, serious motivation aside, we might reinterpret every reference to a physical object arbitrarily as a reference rather to its cosmic complement, the rest of the physical universe. The old names and predicates would be introduced by ostension as usual, but it would be deferred ostension: pointing to what was not part of the intended object. Sensory associations would carry over similarly. The word 'rabbit' would now denote not each rabbit but the cosmic complement of each, and the predicate 'furry' would now denote not each furry thing but the cosmic complement of each. Saying that rabbits are furry would thus be reinterpreted as saying that complements-of-rabbits are complements-of-furry things, with 'complements-of-rabbits' and 'complements-of-furry' seen as atomic predicates. The two sentences are obviously equivalent.

'Cosmic complement of' and 'number table of' express what I call *proxy* functions: one-to-one reinterpretations of objective reference. They leave the truth values of the sentences undisturbed, as these two examples did. It is a matter of reconstruing all terms and predicates as designating or denoting the proxies of what they had designated or denoted. A term that had designated an object x now designates the proxy of x, and a predicate that had denoted x now denotes the proxy of x. No big deal; we are proxying both sides of the predication, and it cancels out. We appreciated the triviality where the proxy was the cosmic complement.

I have stated the matter by reference to one-place predicates. But the many-place predicates must of course be reinterpreted, place by place, in like fashion. Furthermore, any object that is not given a proxy must take itself as proxy, lest it be reused as proxy of another object; that would mar the one-to-one character of the global reinterpretation. Every object in the universe of discourse gets exactly one proxy, and no two objects get the same proxy. The reason such reinterpretations preserve truth values is that they preserve *sameness* of reference from mention to mention throughout discourse. Sameness of reference is what variables mark, and it is all that ontology contributes to science and truth.

The simplest sort of reinterpretation meeting our conditions is mere permutation, redistributing but preserving the ontology. Cosmic complement is an example, if the universe contains those complements as objects to begin with. Spatiotemporal objects are permuted with their complements, and nonspatiotemporal objects are permuted into themselves.

So we have found that a set of sentences can be reinterpreted in any one-to-one way, in respect of the things referred to, without falsifying any of the sentences. Such is ontological relativity, as I have called it, or the indeterminacy of reference. It has indeed been lurking since Chapter III, for we saw there that variables are the bearers of reference and that they only mark sameness thereof.

More particulars are in order regarding this startling ontological triviality. When we reconstrue physical objects as their cosmic complements, what happens to their classes? They get automatically reconstrued through the mandatory reinterpretation of the two-place membership predicate '∈' as applied to physical objects.

For another example we might reconstrue classes themselves across the board, supplanting each by its logical complement and leaving individuals alone. Again the requirement of reinterpreting predicates, in this case the membership predicate again, preserves the truth values of all the sentences. We simply reconstrue it as nonmembership. A familiar and less trivial example at the abstract level is the use of Gödel numbers for strings of signs; one need not care which of the two media one is dealing with.

For abstract objects, F. P. Ramsey was already illustrating the indeterminacy of reference sixty-odd years ago with what we have come to call Ramsey sentences. The underlying thought is that abstract objects serve natural science only through formal laws that we can set down. Certain of those laws might serve one scientific context, and further ones might serve another. The laws needed for either context might not determine those abstract objects uniquely, but no matter. All that matters is that there be some abstract objects or other fulfilling those laws. For instance, there is no end of ways of interpreting natural numbers in set theory, each of which yields classical arithmetic. Ramsey's idea, in the case of natural numbers, is to waive the choice of interpretation and just write an existential quantification to the effect that there is a sequence of abstract objects fulfilling such and such arithmetical laws and functioning thus and so in the desired application.

For a less cumbersome example let us turn to ordered pairs. Let us assume (unrealistically) that we have somehow reached the point of quantifying over functions without taking up ordered pairs. Then occasion arises to affirm something about a pair $\langle u, v \rangle$, and to do so without choosing any one of the various adequate ways of construing ordered pairs. I shall represent the desired sentences about $\langle u, v \rangle$ as '$P\langle u, v \rangle$'. Its Ramsey sentence, then, is

$$\exists f(\forall x \forall y \forall z \forall w$$
$$(fxy = fzw .\equiv. x = z . y = w) . P(fuv)),$$

based on the stipulation (1) of Chapter VI.

Ramsey's treatment thus brings out indeterminacy of reference not by reinterpretation, but by waiving the choice of interpretation. However, the idea does not extend in general to concrete objects. The trouble is that each Ramsey sentence is a fresh existential quantification; consequently there is no assurance of sameness of object from sentence to sentence. In the case of abstract objects, this does not matter: they can be happily dismissed after each application and introduced anew for the next. But for concrete objects—gross bodies, particularly—endurance and identity over time are essential to the very fabric of our spatiotemporal account of things. Thus it is that the structuralism proclaimed by Ramsey was a structuralism of abstract objects, and he claimed no more. My simple argument for indeterminacy of reference is more sweeping, applying as it does to objects indiscriminately. I conclude from it that what matters for any objects, concrete or abstract, is not what they are but what they contribute to our overall theory of the world as neutral nodes in its logical structure.

Having appreciated this point, let us adjust our usage to it rather than bask in paradox. The very freedom vouchsafed us by the indeterminacy of reference allows us to *adopt* ostension as decisive for reference to observable concrete objects. We end up as we began, then, agreeing on the denotations of 'rabbit' after all: rabbits for all concerned. We may then merely differ on the deeper nature of rabbits: they are spatiotemporal regions for some, number tables for others, and sui generis for most. Adaptation of our usage must not, however, be allowed to obscure the lesson of proxy functions. Namely, a language-wide one-to-one reassignment of values to our variables has no effect on the truth or falsity of our statements.

Abstract objects and unobservable concrete ones continue to float free. We had already despaired of making empirical sense of intersubjective identity of unobservables, even before proxy functions reared their ugly heads. Again the very indeterminacy frees us to legislate a criterion, but this time there is nothing evident to go on but smoothness of dialogue and concurrence in conclusions. Ostension is powerless here.

So much for quandaries over reference. Let us look now to meaning. We may settle, with Frege, on whole sentences as the primary vehicles of meaning. The indeterminacy of reference should not interfere with the equating of sentence meanings, taken holophrastically, for we saw that the application of a proxy function to a language leaves the truth conditions of sentences unaffected.

Defining the notion of meaning for sentences may properly be said to consist simply in specifying the circumstances in which two sentences have the same meaning. We can settle for no less, because there is no entity without identity; no meaning without sameness of meaning. And we can require no more, because once we have defined sameness of meaning for sentences we can define the meaning of a sentence by "quasi-analysis" à la Carnap (Chapter I) as the class of all sentences like it in meaning.

In seeking what makes for sameness of meaning of two sentences for a given speaker, we do well to look first to occasion sentences. Some of them are observation sentences, some not, but they all offer what John Stuart Mill called concomitant variation. Sameness of meaning is reflected in sameness of truth value, occasion by occasion. Sameness of meaning of two occasion sentences, then, for a given speaker at a given stage of his development, consists in his then having the *disposition* (Chapter II) to give the same verdict (assent, dissent, abstention) to both sentences on any and every occasion. This is perhaps the most we can require.

The disposition, if there, is a present passive physical state of the subject's nervous system, however little understood, and whether or not activated or otherwise detected. Actually the subject *can* detect it, and he has learned to verbalize it in his unrefined vernacular by saying that the sentences "have the same meaning." Presumably our querying of the two occasion sentences has induced in the subject's imagination the state of mind in which either sentence would come naturally, and he finds both sentences prompted equally. He has acquired the phrase 'have the same meaning' for this form of introspective experience.

Such imagining of scenes and circumstances is central to our every activity, our plans and decisions, from the highly scientific to the most trivial. Our healthy misgivings about introspective psychology must not lead us to underestimate this vital factor, whatever the obscurity of its neural mechanism.

So much for occasion sentences. Regarding standing sentences I see no prospect of a clean-cut concept of sameness of meaning, even for the individual. It comes down to tacit and unsystematic correlations. Various pairs of words are found to be interchangeable in occasion sentences without disturbing sameness of meaning, so their interchange is taken also to preserve meaning of standing sentences. This goes pretty far in equating standing sentences. Some of them may be locked together also by causal regularities. What is in fact a fortuitous mingling of considerations can induce in the speaker's fancy the wraith of a unitary entity, a misty idea or meaning purportedly conveyed indifferently by the two sentences. To transplant Ryle's metaphor, it is the ghost in the machine. For that matter, I think that in standing sentences even the undisciplined layman is apt to betray frequent lack of confidence in ascribing sameness of meaning.

So it is in standing sentences that the notion of meaning goes shaky. But this is the very locus of the philosophical notion of *proposition:* the meaning of a sentence of fixed truth value. Many philosophers have seen propositions as abstract objects that statements served to express. They have seen them as the bearers of truth values; sentences were true and false only in the sense of expressing true and false propositions.

There is indeed a usage of 'proposition' that is useful and unobjectionable. It can be construed as denoting the sentences themselves, rather than their meanings, but it is used instead of 'sentence' when we are concerned with the sentence as an object of belief (as we shall be in Chapter VIII) rather than with its morphology and syntax. I deny myself this convenient usage, for fear of beclouding issues; but it carries no commitment to sentence meanings.

We have now shifted the burden of truth values to the

sentences themselves or, more strictly, to the events of uttering them. It is the individual utterances that matter for occasion sentences—indeed for most of our sentences, where personal pronouns, tensed verbs, and the adverbs 'here', 'there', 'now', and 'then' can make truth value vary with the circumstances of utterance. Still, it is convenient in logical and philosophical contexts to treat sentences rather than their utterances as the truth vehicles, by imagining them filled out with specifications of time, place, and person insofar as needed to freeze their truth values. This fixity restores the convenience that had made propositions attractive.

Thus far we have been reflecting on sameness of meaning of two sentences for one speaker. At the opposite extreme there is the purported sameness of meaning between a sentence of a wildly exotic language and its English translation. Still, the one case is reducible to the other. If time, effort, and money are no object, we can always arrange for a bilingual. The native child acquires complete fluency in his exotic language, and the trained linguist with his varied experience in languages has a head start to the same; so if worst comes to worst, he can become a bilingual on his own.

Given the bilingual, we are back to the single speaker weighing two of his own sentences for sameness of meaning. Again, it works for occasion sentences but is problematic for standing sentences.

It is not a problem of untranslatable sentences. Some will be clearly untranslatable. 'Neutrinos lack mass' is untranslatable into the English of 1930. Nor is it a problem of multiple translatability. Whenever there is an English translation at all, holophrastically acceptable by whatever standard as yet undefined, there will normally be many—namely, all the other English sentences that agree holophrastically in meaning with that one, again by whatever standard as yet undefined. No, it is just the lack of a standard of sameness of meaning itself, within our language or between languages, particularly for standing sentences.

In the hope of glimpsing conditions of sameness of holophrastic meaning in starkest purity, we might follow an anthropological linguist into the wilds, if only in fantasy, and see how he breaks into a native language unrelated to any known one. A native utters something—'Gavagai', of course—just when something salient has occurred, perhaps the scurrying of a rabbit. The linguist guesses that the native's utterance was an observation sentence and that the scurrying prompted it. Both guesses were shaky, but what they conjure up in his mind is the English observation sentence 'Rabbit' or 'Lo, a rabbit'. His conjecture is that if he takes to saying 'Gavagai' in circumstances where he would habitually have said 'Rabbit', it might contribute to his command of the language. Not much, but he is patient.

He accelerates matters by taking the initiative: showing an obliging native a big leaf, a little leaf, a long stick, a short stick, and taking note of the native's utterances in hopes that they denote the displayed objects and their contrast.[1] He amasses observation sentences apace: nouns and adjectives, as he puts it, for he applies familiar grammar where he can.

Observation sentences are thus the entering wedge for the linguist as they were for the child. Further occasion sentences, not observational, would probably be the next in line. They lack the advantage of concurrently observable subject matter, but they retain the advantage of variation under varying conditions. Standing sentences are the stubborn ones: impassive,

1. I am indebted here to one of Kenneth Pike's demonstrations.

inscrutable. It is here, in opportunistic and unsystematic analogies, bold extrapolations, wild guesses, and grasping at straws, that the gifted linguist shows his prowess. What I have called analytical hypotheses come into play. His ascent into the thick of language must resemble the child's, but his groping is less blind because his own language and others in his command afford structures for him to try.

Observation categoricals would no doubt be the first of the standing sentences to yield. Once these are under control, the native idiom for them would no doubt extend directly to the universally quantified conditional without regard to observationality. This should be valuable in suggesting translations of further sentences one after another, since each universal conditional affirms an invariable truth link between two open sentences, one of which may already have been conjecturally translated.

The linguist will rely also on observation of the local folkways. The child does too, but the linguist is a more seasoned observer. Unlike the child, the linguist will not accept everything the native says as true. He will indeed assume sincerity, barring evidence to the contrary, but he will try as an amateur psychologist to fit his interpretations of the native's sentences to the native's likely beliefs rather than to the facts of circumambient nature. Usually the outcome will be the same, since people are so much alike; but his observation of the folkways is his faltering guide to the divergences.

Translation is not the field linguist's goal. His goal is to command the native language and perhaps to teach it, whether for reasons of ethnography and philology or simply to implement fluent dialogue and successful negotiation with the natives. His undertaking, broader than translation, is *interpretation*. An untranslatable sentence, such as the one about neutrinos, can still be interpreted, and that indeed is how we have learned it ourselves. For broadly semantic purposes, as Donald Davidson appreciates, interpretation is the thing. Translation is the narrower project, pertinent specifically to my concern over the fancied concepts of proposition and sameness of meaning.

My consideration of sameness of meaning thus far has concerned sameness for one speaker. I have brought translation under this head by invoking the hypothetical bilingual. This sufficed as a challenge to propositions. But there is also a popular resort to sameness of meaning that calls irreducibly for two speakers, namely in the conception of dialogue as communication of ideas. John Horne Tooke had sought to exorcise ideas and make do with words (Chapter I), but ideas lingered on in the guise of meaning. Meaning is the idea wedded to the word, and as such it is up again for exorcising.

Assessment of intersubjective sameness of meaning presents no problem in observation sentences, since concurrence of witnesses is already a defining condition of observationality. Other occasion sentences are next best, since we can still exploit concomitant variation from occasion to occasion. But they are not as clean a sweep for two speakers as they are for a single speaker, for two speakers might disagree on the truth of an occasion sentence because of a difference in belief rather than meaning (granted the reality of that distinction).

Sometimes one of the speakers can diagnose such a disagreement by switching to another occasion sentence that has the same meaning for him. If the speakers agree on the truth value of this sentence, then clearly the earlier disagreement was semantic; the original sentence did not mean the same for the two speakers, nor did it and its paraphrase mean the same for the second speaker. Often the discrepancy can be narrowed down to a word, by hitting on a substitute that restores agreement.

Such probings pinpoint local divergences in our speech habits without suggesting any coherently definable relation of sameness and difference of meaning between one speaker's sentence and another's. In the case of standing sentences the prospect here is even more desolate, surely, than it was for sameness of meaning of standing sentences for a single individual. It is as hopeless as our earlier question of intersubjective identity of abstract objects.

Our hypothetical bilingual was helpful in reducing the intersubjective to the intrasubjective. What now if two field linguists spent long years going bilingual in the same remote valley while scrupulously shunning each other? Would they agree, in the end, on samenesses of meaning between native standing sentences and English ones? Or suppose they both compiled manuals of translation, and both manuals proved successful in translating some long native monologue into coherent English. Then suppose we translate it again using the two manuals alternately, sentence by sentence. Would the result still be coherent? If not, and given no basis for saying which manual is at fault, we have what I have called indeterminacy of translation.

The practical purpose of such a manual would be inculcation in us of fluency and effectiveness in the native language. The instruction would proceed recursively, for the most part, beginning with the ad hoc pairings of native words with English words and phrases and then explaining grammatical constructions for generating sentences from the words. Translations of most native sentences would be implied, and interpretations of untranslated ones would be provided less systematically. I picture the whole enterprise as directed to the holistic objective of communication.

Similarly for lexicography at home. Though the word 'meaning' is ubiquitous in lexicography, no capital is made of a relation of sameness of meaning. An entry gets broken down into several "meanings" or "senses," so called, but only ad hoc to explain how to use a word in various dissimilar situations. When a word is partly explained by paraphrasing a sample context, as is so often the way, the paraphrase is meant only for typical circumstances, or for specified ones; there is no thought of sameness of meaning in any theoretical sense. Nor does a practical dictionary observe a distinction between linguistic information about a term and factual information about its denotata. The goal is simply the user's success in plying the language.

The word 'meaning' is indeed bandied as freely in lexicography as in the street, and so be it. But let us be wary when it threatens to figure as a supporting member of a theory. In lexicography it does not.

THINGS OF THE MIND

DESCARTES'S ONTOLOGICAL DUALISM of mind and body was not an easy position to rest with. By what mechanism did the one act upon the other? How could such interaction be reconciled with the conservation of energy in the physical world? Granted, what is conserved is now seen to be matter plus energy; but that is no help. Psychophysical parallelism came to be entertained as an escape, but active minds could not long rest with that either.

Monism is now the order of the day. Dualism can be trivially dissolved, if we do not try to allow for disembodied spirits. Every state of mind corresponds to a distinct state of the body, trivially if not otherwise: it corresponds at least, as the dualist must grant, to the bodily state of *having* a mind in that mental state. Acting on this triviality we can simply transfer the mentalistic predicates to the body, bypassing the purported mental substance. We can say of John's body not only that it broke a leg, but that it hurt, and that it thinks it sees how to prove Fermat's Last Theorem. It sounds odd, but philosophically that's all right, outside of midcentury Oxford.

Dualism of substance thus gives way to a mere dualism in the predicates by which we group the states and activities of bodies. Some of the predicates are mentalistic in character, others not.

Effortless monism thus far, form without substance. For the substance of the transaction we turn, as physicalists, to physiology. Pain is a promising example, for neurologists no doubt understand its neural mechanism to a considerable degree, and pain can be identified with that. If there are several alternative mechanisms, we can take their alternation. Whatever can be said about pain can be so rephrased as to be said about its mechanism. Where '*Fx*' means that *x* is a dull ache, we reinterpret *x* as the neural mechanism and then reinterpret '*Fx*' compensatorially as 'the pain *that* x *produces* is a dull ache'. The logic is simply that of proxy functions (Chapter VII).

These reflections on pain apply equally to sensations and emotions generally, granted our physicalistic conviction that each of these has its distinctive mechanism or set of alternative mechanisms. But what if the mechanisms differ from person to person? The physicalist would be astonished, but he would rally. He might just say that pain is a state of an individual's nerves that tends to be manifested by writhing and wincing and to be caused by strains, bruises, lesions, and the like. Correspondingly for other sensations and, less easily, the emotions.

The reduction of the mental to the physical, or indeed of arithmetic to set theory, can be characterized in either of two ways: as *explaining* or as explaining *away*. There is no difference, but the first phrasing has a gentler ring. To have *repudiated* the life of the mind seems harsher than to have *explained* it in physical terms.

In some domains the harsher phrasing is better, notably in the various ways of defining natural numbers in set theory. For Frege, twelve was (nearly enough) the class of all dozens; for von Neumann it was the class of the first twelve natural numbers, from zero through eleven. It cannot be both. We can resolve the dilemma by not identifying twelve with either. We can do without the natural numbers; their work can be done by Frege's classes or, equally, by von Neumann's. We proceed to use one or the other set of surrogates, or some third, and conveniently call the surrogates by the newly vacated numerical names. We have solved the puzzle by speaking of *alternative eliminations* rather than *conflicting explanations*. But there is no real difference between the two characterizations.

A similar but less famous example to the same effect is the ordered pair (Chapter VI), with its various inequivalent definitions to the same practical effect.

Assimilation of the mental to the physical, however, invites the gentler phrasing: the mental is *explained* in physical terms. Phrased either way, the assimilation seems reasonable as applied to pain and other sensations and emotions. Where it perhaps seems less compélling is in application to thinking. The notion of an exhaustive class of states each of which qualifies as thinking about Fermat's Last Theorem, and each of which is specifiable in purely physiological terms, seems discouragingly unrealistic even if restricted to a single thinker. It is at this point that we must perhaps acquiesce in the psychophysical dualism of predicates, though clinging to our effortless monism of substance. It is what Davidson has called *anomalous monism*. Each occurrence of a mental state is still, we insist, an occurrence of a physical state of a body, but the groupings of these occurrences under mentalistic predicates are largely untranslatable into physiological terms. There is token identity, to give it the jargon, but type diversity.

The general predicate 'thinking about Fermat's Last Theorem', then, is irreducibly mentalistic. It still denotes various physical objects in its intermittent way (usually mathematicians), and it has its place in our meaningful physicalistic language. The point of anomalous monism is just that our mentalistic predicate imposes on bodily states and events a grouping that cannot be defined in the special vocabulary of physiology. Each of those individual states and events is physiologically describable, we presume, given all pertinent information.

Some of the activity of thinking is in the brain and some apparently in the muscles. Recent developments in computer theory under the name of *connectionism* are believed to simulate much of what goes on in the brain. Imagine a plate in the brain with nerves leading to it from all sensory receptors. Each nerve has its separate terminal on the plate. Then imagine a second plate with nerves leading out from it to all motor muscles. Finally imagine nerves linking each terminal on the one plate with each terminal on the other. Activation of any one of these links makes it more sensitive to further activation. Such is believed to be the mechanism of conditioning, habituation, expectation; not quite thought, but its substructure.

For a more faithful model, imagine many intervening plates, each similarly cross-linked to the next. What makes the model promising is that computers so designed make predictions. Biases that the engineers build into the designs play the role of the human subject's innate standards of perceptual similarity (Chapter II).[1]

When we deliberately and effortfully think, presumably muscles come into play. Primary among these are the speech muscles; for thought, as John B. Watson claimed, is primarily incipient speech. Thinking aloud is just uninhibited thinking. Other muscles enter the thought process too, as Watson appreciated, notably in the case of the artist or acrobat who plans

---

1. On connectionism see Churchland, pp. 159–188.

his moves with incipient rehearsals of muscular involvement, or the engineer, who simulates in his muscles the lay of the land or the distribution of stresses in what he means to build. The artist, engineer, and acrobat are poor at putting their thoughts into words, for they were thinking with nonverbal muscles.

Acrobat, artist, and engineer notwithstanding, language and thought have been tightly joined down the ages. The signals of the birds and apes evolved as a means of reporting perceptions when there was perhaps little else in the way of thought to report. As language went on developing in early man, its capacity to communicate increased; and conversely the proliferation of thought worth communicating was itself due to the development of language. Language was creating its own cargo.

Perception of another's unspoken thought, however—up to a point—is older than language. Empathy is instinctive. Child psychologists tell us that an infant just a few days old responds to an adult's facial expression, even to imitating it by the unlearned flexing of appropriate muscles. Dogs and bears are believed to detect fear and anger in people and other animals, perhaps by smell.

Empathy figures also in the child's acquisition of his first observation sentences. He does not just hear the sentence, see the reported object or event, and then associate the two. He also notes the speaker's orientation, gesture, and facial expression. In his as yet inarticulate way he perceives that the speaker perceives the object or event. When the child puts the sentence to use, there is again a perceiving of perceiving, this time in reverse. The listener, concerned with the child's progress, takes note of his orientation and facial expression. The listener is not satisfied by mere truth of the utterance; the child has to have perceived its truth to win applause.

'Perceives that', followed by an observation sentence as subordinate clause, is thus a construction that is implicit, if only tacit, in the learning of language and the handing down of it from generation to generation. I see it as in effect the primeval idiom for ascribing a thought. A further idiom to the purpose, no longer directed to a child's observation sentence, is 'It occurred to him that'. ('He thought that' will not quite do, because of an odd twist of English usage: we use this to report not an episode of thinking but a state of believing.)

All three of these idioms—'perceives that', 'thinks that', 'It occurred to him that'—are idioms of so-called *propositional attitude*. Others of them are 'believes that', 'doubts, expects, hopes, fears, regrets that'; also indeed 'says, denies, predicts, strives that', although these last four, like 'perceives that' and 'It occurred to him that', report acts or events rather than attitudes.

As they stand, the idioms of propositional attitude resist predicate logic. They embed one sentence in another in a way irresoluble into truth functions and quantification. Their underlying trait, which pervades mentalistic talk pretty generally, is that they are *intensional*, whereas predicate logic is extensional.

A context is *extensional* if its truth value cannot be changed by supplanting a component sentence by another of the same truth value, nor by supplanting a component predicate by another with all the same denotata, nor by supplanting a singular term by another with the same designatum. Succinctly, the three requirements are substitutivity of *covalence*, of *coextensiveness*, and of *identity, salva veritate*. A context is *intensional* if it is not extensional.

Extensionality is much of the glory of predicate logic, and it is much of the glory of any science that can be grammatically embedded in predicate logic. I find extensionality necessary, indeed, though not sufficient, for my full understanding of a theory. In particular it is an affront to common sense to see a true sentence go false when a singular term in it is supplanted by another that names the same thing. What is true of a thing is true of it, surely, under any name.

It is violation of this third requirement, substitutivity of identity, that we find most offensive. Might we still look kindly on contexts that meet the third requirement but violate the other two? No; the three requirements interlock inseparably. To see how substitutivity of identity virtually assures substitutivity of coextensiveness, let 'F' and 'G' represent two coextensive one-place predicates. The classes of their respective denotata are identical: $\{x: Fx\} = \{x: Gx\}$. Now the immediate context of 'F' in any sentence is 'Fa' where 'a' represents some variable or singular term; and 'Fa' is set-theoretically equivalent to '$a \in \{x: Fx\}$', which, in view of the substitutivity of identity, can be replaced *salva veritate* by '$a \in \{x: Gx\}$', which is logically equivalent to 'Ga'. 'G' can thus supplant 'F' in any context *salva veritate*. Substitutivity of coextensiveness is fulfilled.

In this reasoning I have made two tacit assumptions, but they are minor. One is that set-theoretic equivalence is substitutive *salva veritate*. The other is the existence of $\{x: Fx\}$, which fails in paradoxical cases such as Russell's $\{x: x \notin x\}$.

The argument from the substitutivity of identity to the substitutivity of coextensiveness carries over to the substitutivity of covalence, since statements 'p' and 'q' are covalent if and only if $\{x: p . x = x\} = \{x: q . x = x\}$.

The intensionality of the propositional attitudes is evident at every turn. Substitutivity of identity is breached as soon as we reflect, with Russell, that His Majesty was unaware that Scott was the author of *Waverley;* for the majesty in question was indeed aware that Scott was Scott, and in point of historical fact Scott was indeed the author of *Waverley*. The source of the difficulty is equally evident: a discrepancy between the world as grasped by the man in the propositional attitude—the *attitudinist,* let us call him—and the world as known to the reporter of the attitude and the rest of us. This accounts for the failures of substitutivity of identity: the attitudinist was unaware of the identity. It accounts also for the failures of substitutivity of coextensiveness and covalence: the attitudinist was simply wrong about the truth values of the sentences or the denotata of the predicates concerned.

For coping with these discrepancies and reconciling them with our tried and true extensional logic, the reasonable expedient is a syntactic barrier between the world as conceived by the attitudinist and the world as we intend it. How to erect this barrier is already suggested by our traditional grammar of propositional attitudes, namely the encapsulating of sentences, as 'that' clauses, within sentences. We have merely to fortify the 'that' as a firm barrier; for it is passage across the 'that' that persists in breaching extensionality.

Orthographically the strategy is to strengthen the conjunction 'that' to an unequivocal quotation mark. The move is what I call *semantic ascent:* mentioning an expression by name instead of using it as a component clause. The quotation is a name strictly of the sequence of characters depicted within it, or the associated sequence of phonemes, so the quoted words have no semantic or syntactic bearing on the outlying text. The attitudinal verbs 'believes', 'doubts', 'expects', 'hopes', 'regrets', 'says', 'denies', 'perceives', and 'strives' become two-place predicates relating attitudinists to sentences. The attitudinist need not speak the language of the sentence, nor any language. The sentence is provided by the ascriber of the attitude, and it is a sentence that comes naturally to him when he imagines himself in what he takes to be the attitudinist's situation and attitude. He phrases the sentence with a view not to what exists in the real world and what predicates or sentences are really coextensive or covalent, but rather with a view to what he takes the attitudinist to believe. Hence the breaches of extensionality when the attitudinal sentence clashes with outer discourse. Happily the quotation marks seal it off.

An effect is that believing, doubting, hoping, expecting, regretting, and the rest come to be treated as relations between people and sentences. Creatures other than people also may qualify. This recasting is not even unnatural in the case of believing, and anyway, as already remarked, unnaturalness in philosophy is all right.

Even philosophical license, however, cannot condone the further step of identifying beliefs, doubts, hopes, expectations, and regrets with the sentences believed, doubted, hoped, expected, regretted. Sentences differ, if merely in phrasing or spelling, though beliefs be reckoned identical. We speak of shared beliefs and of sameness of belief where the sentences vary fairly freely. Individuation of beliefs, and therewith reification of beliefs, is of a piece with the individuation and reification of meanings, ideas, properties, and propositions. All these are *entia non grata* by my lights, and similarly for doubts, hopes, expectations, regrets. But believing, doubting, hoping, expecting, regretting, all continue alive and well, and *their* objects, by *my* lights, are sentences.

The foregoing strictures apply also to thoughts in one of two senses. Thinking is a bodily activity in good standing, however inadequate our physiological understanding of it. The acts of thinking—the *thoughts* in one sense of the term—are justly reified. I would say the same of perceptions, as events. But thoughts in the other sense, identifiable and distinguishable thought contents, I despair of accommodating.

One propositional attitude, *saying,* raises a minor point of usage. The attitudinal idiom is 'says that', and the ensuing sentence does not pretend to directness of quotation; but our new artifice of treating 'that' as quotation does replicate the standard idiom of direct quotation. There is no difficulty here. We are not promoting a revision of traditional usage, but only reinterpreting it. Old editorial guidelines remain in place. If we were to implement the reinterpretation with a revised style sheet, we could just settle for two verbs: 'says' for the propositional attitude and 'utters' for the direct quotation, with quotation marks for both.

There is a shortsighted but stubborn notion that a mere string of marks on paper cannot be true, false, doubted, or believed. Of course it can, because of conventions relating it to speech habits and because of neural mechanisms linking speech habits causally to mental activity.[2] Less naively, linguists protest that a sentence is more than a string of characters or phonemes; the same string can represent now one sentence and now a grammatically or semantically different sentence, through homonymy. A sentence, they insist, is a string coupled with a syntactic or semantic tree. Now this is all very well except for the insistence. It may well be the efficient terminology for working empirical linguists, and I wish them Godspeed; but it is precisely the contrary for philosophers or psychologists of language. The terminology presupposes the very connections and distinctions that most concern them. Different pursuits call for different jargons, however homonymous.

Quotation has made the propositional attitudes safe for extensional logic (except for propositional attitudes *de re*, whereof anon). The quotation is just a name of the depicted sequence

2. See "Foreword, 1980" in the 1980 printing of my *From a Logical Point of View.*

of letters and spaces, dissociated grammatically and semantically from the outlying text. The dissociation becomes still more graphic when we analyze the quotation explicitly into names of the individual characters and spaces, linked by concatenation signs. The Greek alphabet affords vivid illustration, thanks to the robust names of the letters:

'παντα ρει =
pi‿alpha‿nu‿tau‿alpha‿space‿rho‿epsilon‿iota.

We have a familiar word for this analysis of quotation: it is *spelling*. Spelled out, the words disappear and so do questions of substitutivity. Substitutivity within quotation is confusion of use with mention.

Spelling is important in dispelling a strange misconception, which I have encountered occasionally, that a quotation relates to its context as an irreducibly single component word. On the contrary, spelling resolves a quotation into a structured compound as articulate as a polynomial.

In passing, a word now about the ontology of expressions, that is, of strings of characters and spaces. One's first thought is to identify the expression with the class of all its tokens, or concrete inscriptions, past and future. This will not do, for then all expressions that never happened to get written down, and never will, would reduce indiscriminately to the empty class. There are generalities in syntax and semantics that depend rather on there being a distinct new expression for every concatenation of old ones, however long and uninstantiated.

The individual characters present no such problem, for tokens of each exist in profusion. A character can still be construed as the class of its tokens. A string of characters, then, can be explained as the mathematical *sequence* (Chapter VI) of its component characters. It exists as a distinct abstract object regardless of what tokens of it may or may not ever get written down.

Quotation, then, neatly defined by spelling, marks the boundary between the ascriber's impersonation of the attitudinist and the ascriber's speaking for himself. Now and again, however, the ascriber interrupts his empathy and interjects reality, by his own lights, into the attitudinist's world. He says there is someone whom Ralph believes to be a spy; someone in the ascriber's real world, irrespective of how Ralph's attitudinal world may be populated. He declares that

(1) $\exists x$(Ralph believes that x is a spy),

thus affirming the existence, in the real world, of a suspect in Ralph's world. How the cross-identification? Maybe there are two people whom Ralph has taken to be one. Maybe there is one whom he has taken to be two, suspecting the one while trusting the other. A virtue of our treatment was that it sealed off the two worlds, obviating such collision of incompatible ontologies. On our treatment, indeed, (1) becomes

(2) $\exists x$(Ralph believes 'x is a spy'),

which simply misses the point. Its quantification is vacuous, for the recurrence of 'x' disappears altogether in favor of a name of the letter when the quotation is spelled out.

Blithe dismissal of (1), even so, is not easy. Between (1) and the impeccable

(3)   Ralph believes that $\exists x$(x is a spy)

there is all the difference between information pertinent to national security and information too banal to be worth imparting.

The difference, we are told, is that in the case of (1) Ralph knows who the pertinent value of 'x' is. He can specify him by a singular description. This answer was effectively refuted by Robert Sleigh, who offered the singular description 'the shortest spy'. Just grant Ralph the plausible hypothesis that there are no two shortest, and you have him fulfilling (1) without harboring any information less trivial than in (3).

Ascriptions such as (1), which breach the barrier between the ascriber's real world and the fancied world of the attitudinist, are called ascriptions of propositional attitude *de re*. The others are *de dicto*. The expedient of taking sentences as the objects of the attitudes, which achieved extensionality, works only for the attitudes *de dicto*. In 1956 my line, nearly enough, was to extensionalize the attitudes *de re* by according them multiple objects, namely predicates together with persons or other things. Thus (1) would become

$$\exists x(\text{Ralph believes 'is a spy' of } x).$$

However, Sleigh's example suggests that the attitudes *de re* have no distinctive content worth trying to accommodate.

There is no denying that (1) sounds an alert to security agents and (3) does not; but the features distinguishing (1) from (3) may vary too irregularly with the details of the situation to admit of formal encapsulation without encapsulating the shortest spy along with them. 'Knowing who he is' can sometimes mean knowing his face but not his name, sometimes knowing his name but not his face, sometimes knowing both but not his social significance, sometimes knowing where to find him; so generalizing to singular description covers too much.

One line open to us is to omit propositional attitudes *de re* from our overall scientific language couched in the extensional grammar of predicate logic, but to value them still as informative leads. The security agent is indeed alerted by (1) and proceeds to question Ralph, recording his testimony in ascriptions *de dicto* properly suited to the scientific framework. We are familiar with other such outriders of the scientific enterprise, notably the indexical idioms involving demonstratives, tenses, and personal pronouns, to say nothing of occasion sentences generally, observational and otherwise.

Howard Burdick has taken a more heroic line on the *de re* attitudes. He posits an apparatus of tacit predicates as parameters appropriate to the particular occasion on which the attitude is ascribed. Through an ingenious and elaborate construction he succeeds in accommodating the attitudes *de re* in the extensional framework.

Either way, the conspicuously intensional idiom of propositional attitude finds its niche. In the first way, propositional attitudes *de dicto* find their place within the overall language of science, and the attitudes *de re* find theirs as extraneous aids. In the second way, Burdick's, both kinds end up within.

In either case the language is extensional but includes mentalistic predicates by courtesy of anomalous monism. The verbs of propositional attitude mostly remain mentalistic: not presumed translatable into physiological terms, though each individual mental event purports to be physiologically specifiable. Such is the extensionalist accommodation of the erstwhile intensional idioms of propositional attitude.

Another recalcitrant idiom, less readily dispensable than the *de re* attitudes and presenting similar problems, is the subjunctive or contrary-to-fact conditional. Here again my inclination is to set it outside the systematic fabric of science as a useful outrider. Alternatively, it might submit to an extension of Burdick's method. Either way it is the indispensable vehicle of thought experiment.

Another notoriously intensional slough is the modal logic

of necessity. Insofar as sense is to be made of necessity, I would sustain extensionality by adopting again the strategy we applied to propositional attitudes *de dicto,* namely semantic ascent. The modal adverb 'necessarily', governing a subordinate sentence, gives way to the predicate 'necessary,' governing a quotation of that sentence.

As in (2) above, so again here, an effect of the semantic ascent is that we can no longer effectively quantify into the affected clause from outside. Modal logic loses therewith most of its punch, but in my eyes this is no loss; for in my extensionalism I make no sense of necessity as a concept of science or philosophy. The adverb 'necessarily' is useful indeed, but only as an expository guide. It marks a sentence as one on which the interlocutor presumably agrees, or which follows from something farther up the page, as distinct from points still under debate or in process of being proved. I see it as an extraneous aid on a par with the indexicals and perhaps the contrafactuals and the propositional attitudes *de re.*

Necessity and possibility are interdefinable duals like '$\forall$' and '$\exists$': 'possibly' means 'not necessarily not'. My cavalier treatment of the one, then, carries over to the other. Probability, however, is quote another matter. Subjective probability is degree of belief. It dominates the normative side of naturalized epistemology, as noted at the end of Chapter IV. It is a quantitative refinement of a propositional attitude and admits of formulation *de dicto* with the help of quotation in the manner of the other propositional attitudes.

✤ APPENDIX ✤
PREDICATE FUNCTORS

THE PREDICATE FUNCTORS hark back to Moses Schönfinkel's combinatory functions (1924). These, like predicate functors, analyzed the variable by eliminating it. This was Schönfinkel's great achievement. However, his functions afforded a
notation for a full set theory and faced the usual challenge of
Russell's and other paradoxes. Haskell Curry devoted a career
to developing a consistent set theory in Schönfinkel's terms.

Schönfinkel's combinatory functions owe their inordinate
power to their being functions applicable to functions; hence
applicable to themselves and one another. Predicate functors,
on the other hand, are mere adverbs, attaching to predicates
(verbs, adjectives, . . .) to modify them into further, more
complex predicates. It is in predicate functors that the analysis
of the variable is extricated from set-theoretic entanglements
and rendered coextensive with elementary logic.

In a lecture of 1957, published in 1959, Paul Bernays presented a system of predicate functors superimposed on truth-
function logic and covering quantification. Independently in
my 1959 note "Eliminating variables . . . ," which I expanded
to "Variables explained away," I presented a set of predicate
functors whose output just coincided with the truth functions
and quantification.

The sets of primitive predicate functors have varied in subsequent publications, but with the same net output: the truth functions and quantification. The present set of six is unusual in its economy. Bernays had acquiesced in an infinity of permutation functors. I had got them down to two. It was George Myro who showed me in 1971 that a single one, 'Perm', could be made to suffice with the aid of my '∃' and 'Pad', which I needed anyway.[1]

In the remaining pages I shall show how any *closed* formula of quantification theory can be translated into a formula composed of our six or fewer predicate functors in application to various of our schematic letters 'F^0', 'G^0', . . . , 'F^1', . . . , 'G^1', . . . , 'F^2', ... I shall continue to omit these exponents when variables are still attached. By 'closed', above, I mean devoid of free variables; and I mean 'quantification theory' to cover truth functions and quantification but not identity. Identity can be added to both quantification logic and predicate-functor logic when wanted.

To begin with let us come to terms with parentheses. In an iteration, for example, in

$$(\mathrm{Perm}(\mathrm{Pad}(\exists(\mathrm{Refl}(\mathrm{Perm}\ F)))))xyxzw,$$

the internal parentheses are redundant. Since predicate functors apply only to predicates and not to one another, no other grouping would have made sense. Our example becomes

$$(\mathrm{Perm\ Pad\ \exists\ Refl\ Perm}\ F)xyxzw.$$

Consider now the infinite lot of *retrojection* functors 'Ret_i' such that

$$(\mathrm{Ret}_i\ F)x_i x_1 x_2 \ldots x_{i-1} x_{i+1} \ldots x_n \equiv F x_1 \ldots x_n.$$

---

1. For more history see my *Ways of Paradox*, enlarged edition, pp. 283–321.

Applied to an n-place predicate, it throws the ith argument back to the initial position. 'Ret$_2$', applied to a two-place predicate, is our familiar conversion functor; applied to 'parent of' or 'greater than', it gives 'child of' or 'less than'. 'Ret$_1$' is useless; it leaves things alone.

Now what Myro showed me was that 'Ret$_i$ F^n' is definable as

$$\text{Perm } (n-i \text{ times}) \ \exists \ \text{Perm } (i-1 \text{ times}) \ \text{Pad } F^n.$$

The reasoning is as follows.

$Fx_1 \ldots x_n$ [$(\text{Pad } F)x_0 \ldots x_n$
$\equiv (\text{Perm Pad } F)x_0 x_2 \ldots x_n x_1$
$\equiv (\text{Perm Perm Pad } F)x_0 x_3 \ldots x_n x_1 x_2$

. . .

$\equiv (\text{Perm } (i-1 \text{ times}) \ \text{Pad } F)x_0 x_i \ldots x_n x_1 \ldots x_{i-1}$
$\equiv (\exists \ \text{Perm } (i-1 \text{ times}) \ \text{Pad } F)x_i \ldots x_n x_1 \ldots x_{i-1}$
$\equiv (\text{Perm } \exists \ \text{Perm } (i-1 \text{ times}) \ \text{Pad } F)$
$\qquad\qquad x_i x_{i+2} \ldots x_n x_1 \ldots x_{i-1} x_{i+1}$

. . .

$\equiv (\text{Perm } (n-i \text{ times}) \ \exists \ \text{Perm } (i-1 \text{ times}) \ \text{Pad } F)$
$\qquad\qquad x_i x_1 \ldots x_{i-1} x_{i+1} \ldots x_n$

The importance of retrojection is that it enables us to rearrange a string of variables in any desired order. We begin by retrojecting the variable that we want to come last in the new order, then we retroject the one that we want to come next to last, and so on. For example, given some predicate 'F^5', suppose we want to form a super-converse 'G^5' of 'F^5' such that $Gvxwzy \equiv Fvwxyz$.

$Fvwxyz \equiv (\text{Ret}_4 F)yvwxz$
$\qquad\quad \equiv (\text{Ret}_5 \text{Ret}_4 F)zyvwx$
$\qquad\quad \equiv (\text{Ret}_4 \text{Ret}_5 \text{Ret}_4 F)wzyvx$

$$\equiv (\text{Ret}_5\text{Ret}_4\text{Ret}_5\text{Ret}_4 F)xwzyv$$
$$\equiv (\text{Ret}_5\text{Ret}_5\text{Ret}_4\text{Ret}_5\text{Ret}_4 F)vxwzy.$$

Duplications can be eliminated from a string of variables by retrojecting duplicate pairs and applying 'Refl'. Idle new variables can be prefixed by 'Pad'. Afterward, as we saw, we can rearrange the string as we please by the retrojection functors. By these means always, and often more briefly by others, we can *homogenize* any two predications; that is, endow them with matching strings of variables, free of repetitions. For example, the heterogeneous *'Fwzwxy'* and *'Gvxyz'* are verifiably equivalent respectively to the homogeneous ones

$$(\text{Pad Refl Perm } F)vwxyz, \qquad (\text{Ret}_2 \text{ Pad } G)vwxyz.$$

Now we can proceed to translate any given closed formula of quantification theory into predicate functors, as follows. Translate universal quantification into existential quantification and negation in the familiar way, and all truth functions into negation and conjunction. Put exponents on the predicate letters according to how many variables are attached, and change any sentence letters *'p'*, *'q'*, etc. to *'F⁰'*, *'G⁰'*, etc. If a variable is repeated in a predication, delete the duplicate by 'Ret' and 'Refl'. Wherever a predication is negated, apply the negation sign rather to the predicate as a complement sign. Wherever two predications occur in conjunction, homogenize them and then render their conjunction as a predication of the intersection of the predicates; for,

$$F^n x_1 \ldots x_n \;.\; G^n x_1 \ldots x_n \equiv (F^n G^n)x_1 \ldots x_n.$$

Continuing thus, we reduce each innermost quantification to an existential quantification of a single predication. Its predicate will be complex, usually, built up of predicate letters by our functors; and now we further complicate it by applying a retrojection functor to bring the quantified variable into initial position. The quantification becomes '$\exists x \; \Gamma x y_1 \ldots y_n$', say, where '$\Gamma$' stands for some complex predicate. Our earlier clearing of repetitions assures us that the 'x' has no further occurrences in the predication, so we can now drop 'x' altogether and treat the quantifier as the cropping functor: '$(\exists \Gamma) y_1 \ldots y_n$'. The bound variable '$x$' is no more. As the translation continues, quantifications that were not innermost become so and are rid of their quantified variables in turn. Our closed sentence schema of quantification theory ends up as a complex zero-place predicate schema composed of predicate functors and predicate letters.[2]

2. This last long paragraph is cribbed in large part from page 287 of my *Methods of Logic,* 4th ed.

❧ REFERENCES ❧

Bentham, Jeremy. *See* Ogden.

Bernays, Paul. "Ueber eine natürliche Erweiterung des Relationenkalküls," in A. Heyting, ed., *Constructivity in Mathematics* (Amsterdam: North Holland, 1959), 1–14.

Bickerton, Derek. *The Roots of Language.* Ann Arbor: Karoma, 1981.

Boole, George. *See* MacHale.

Burdick, Howard. "A logical form for propositional attitudes," *Synthese* 52 (1982), 185–230.

Carnap, Rudolf. *Der logische Aufbau der Welt.* Berlin, 1928. Translation by R. A. George, *The Logical Structure of the World.* Berkeley: University of California Press, 1967.

Churchland, Paul. *A Neurocomputational Perspective.* Cambridge, Mass.: MIT Press, 1989.

Curry, H. B. *Combinatory Logic.* Amsterdam: North Holland. Vol. I (with Robert Feys), 1958; Vol. II (with J. R. Hindley and J. P. Seldin), 1972.

Davidson, Donald. *Essays on Action and Events* (especially Essays 11–12). Oxford: Clarendon, 1980.

———. *Inquiries into Truth and Interpretation* (especially Essays 9–11). Oxford: Clarendon, 1984.

Frege, Gottlob. *Die Grundlagen der Arithmetik.* Breslau, 1884. Translation by J. L. Austin, *The Foundations of Arithmetic.* New York: Harper, 1960.

Geach, P. T. *Reference and Generality,* 2nd ed. Ithaca: Cornell University Press, 1980.

Gödel, Kurt. "Die Vollständigkeit der Axiome des logischen Funktionenkalküls," *Monatshefte für Mathematik und Physik* 37 (1930), 349–360. Translated in van Heijenoort.

————. "Ueber formal unentscheidbare Sätze der *Principia Mathematica* und verwandter Systeme," *Monatshefte für Mathematik und Physik* 38 (1931), 173–198. Translated in van Heijenoort.

Grelling, Kurt, and Leonhard Nelson. "Bemerkungen zu den Paradoxien von Russell und Burali-Forti," *Abhandlungen der Fries'schen Schule* 2 (1907–1908), 300–334.

Jeffrey, Richard. *The Logic of Decision.* New York: McGraw-Hill, 1965.

Kuratowski, Kazimierz. "Sur la notsion de l'ordre dans la théorie des ensembles," *Fundamenta Mathematicae* 2 (1921), 161–171.

Lambek, Karel. *See* Skyrms and Lambert.

MacHale, Desmond. *George Boole: His Life and Work.* Dublin: Boole Press, 1985.

Mill, J. S. *A System of Logic.* 2 vols. London, 1868.

Morgenstern, Oskar. *See* von Neumann and Morgenstern.

Ogden, C. K. *Bentham's Theory of Fictions.* London: Routledge, 1982.

Peano, Giuseppe. *Formulaire de mathématiques,* 3rd ed. Paris, 1901.

Peirce, C. S. *Collected Papers.* 8 vols. Cambridge, Mass.: Harvard University Press, 1931–1958.

Piaget, Jean. *Genetic Epistemology.* New York: Columbia University Press, 1970.

Quine, W. V. *From a Logical Point of View.* Cambridge, Mass.: Harvard University Press, 1953; 2nd ed., rev., 1980.

————. "Eliminating variables without applying functions to functions" (abstract). *Journal of Symbolic Logic* 24 (1959), 324–325.

————. "Variables explained away." *Proceedings of American Philosophical Society* 104 (1960), 343–347. Reprinted in Quine, *Selected Logic Papers.* New York, 1965; enlarged ed., Cambridge, Mass.: Harvard University Press, 1995.

————. *The Ways of Paradox and Other Essays,* rev. and enlarged ed. Cambridge, Mass.: Harvard University Press, 1976.

————. *Methods of Logic,* 4th ed. Cambridge, Mass.: Harvard University Press, 1982.

Ramsey, F. P. *The Foundations of Mathematics and Other Logical Essays.* London, 1931.

Russell, Bertrand. *The Principles of Mathematics.* Cambridge, Eng., 1903.

————. "On denoting." *Mind* 14 (1905), 479–493.

————. *Our Knowledge of the External World.* New York and London, 1914.

————. *See also* Whitehead and Russell.

Schönfinkel, Moses. "Ueber die Bausteine der mathematischen Logik," *Mathematische Annalen* 92 (1924), 305–316. Translated in van Heijenoort.

Skyrms, Brian, and Karel Lambert. "Resiliency and laws in the web of belief." Forthcoming.

Sleigh, Robert. "On a proposed system of epistemic logic," *Noûs* 2 (1968), 391–398.

Tarski, Alfred. "The concept of truth in formalized languages," in his *Logic, Semantics, Metamathematics,* Oxford, 1956, and Indianapolis: Hackett, 1983, pp. 152–278. Translated from the German of 1935–36 by J. H. Woodger.

Tooke, John Horne. "Επεα πτερόεντα, or, *The Diversions of Purley,* vol. 1. London, 1786; Boston, 1806.

van Heijenoort, Jean, ed. *From Frege to Gödel: A Source Book in Mathematical Logic, 1879–1931.* Cambridge, Mass.: Harvard University Press, 1967.

von Neumann, John. "Zur Einführung der transfiniten Zahlen," *Acta Litterarum ac Scientiarum Regiae Universitatis Hungaricae Francisco-Josephinae* (sectio scientiarum-mathematicarum) 1 (1923), 199–208. Translated in van Heijenoort.

von Neumann, John, and Oskar Morgenstern. *Theory of Games and Economic Behavior.* Princeton: Princeton University Press, 1947.

Watson, J. B. *Psychology from the Standpoint of a Behaviorist.* Philadelphia, 1919.

Whitehead, A. N., and B. Russell. *Principia Mathematica.* 3 vols. Cambridge, Eng., 1910–1913.

Wiener, Norbert. "A simplification of the logic of relations." *Proceedings of Cambridge Philosophical Society* 17 (1912–14), 387–390.

❧ INDEX ❧

DATE DUE

		JAN 0 9 2004	
	FEB 1 0 1996		
	NOV 2 1 2000		
	FEB 0 5 2003		
GAYLORD			PRINTED IN U.S.A.